books designed with giving in mind

The Ground Beef Cookbook	Kid's Arts and Crafts	Natural Foods
Cocktails & Hors d'Oeuvres	Bread Baking	Chinese Vegetarian
Salads & Casseroles	The Crockery Pot Cookbook	The Jewish Cookbook
Kid's Party Book	Kid's Garden Book	Working Couples
Pressure Cooking	Classic Greek Cooking	Mexican
Food Processor Cookbook	The Compleat American	Sunday Breakfast
Peanuts & Popcorn	Housewife 1776	Fisherman's Wharf Cookbook
Kid's Pets Book	Low Carbohydrate Cookbook	Charcoal Cookbook
Make It Ahead	Kid's Cookbook	Ice Cream Cookbook
French Cooking	Italian	Blender Cookbook
Soups & Stews	Cheese Guide & Cookbook	The Wok, a Chinese Cookbook
Crepes & Omelets	Miller's German	Cast Iron Cookbook
Microwave Cooking	Quiche & Souffle	Japanese Country
Vegetable Cookbook	To My Daughter, With Love	Fondue Cookbook

from nitty gritty productions

With love to a special friend:

Linda Holmes Kralik

THE CROCKERY POT COOKBOOK

by LOU SEIBERT PAPPAS

Illustrated by MIKE NELSON

© Copyright 1975
Nitty Gritty Productions
Concord, California

A Nitty Gritty Book*
Published by
Nitty Gritty Productions
P.O. Box 5457
Concord, California 94524

*Nitty Gritty Books - Trademark
Owned by Nitty Gritty Productions
Concord, California

ISBN 0-911954-11-2

Library of Congress Catalog Card Number: 75-9644

Library of Congress Cataloging in Publication Data

Pappas, Lou Seibert.
   The crockery pot cookbook.

   Includes index.
   1. Cookery.   2. Casserole recipes.
I.   Title.
TX652.P28   641.5'86   75-9644
ISBN 0-911954-11-2

CONTENTS

INTRODUCTION

Once you have used a crockery-lined, slow electric cooker it is easy to understand why they are so popular. It's like having a "genie" at home cooking while you're away. When you arrive home, delicious food is waiting and there's no preparation mess to clean up. THAT was all done earlier in the day! It creates a note of serenity in the kitchen. You are free and clear to relax a few minutes and there's even time for an aperitif. Dinner waits without fear of scorching or drying out.

Because the crockery pot concept calls for long cooking, it forces the master of the kitchen to organize in advance. It means you get set for dinner early in the day rather than relying on something fast in the evening. Many working women make some of the necessary preparations, such as cutting up meat and organizing the other ingredients, the evening before. Putting the recipe together the next morning takes only a few minutes. The crockery pot is turned on and dinner is on its way. It's a great way to prepare meals. Food cooked this slow method retains more vitamins and minerals so it is extra nutritious, too.

Slow cooking, made possible by low temperature, is the key to the fine flavor, juiciness and lack of shrinkage you achieve, especially with meats and poultry. Most, if not all, of the stoneware-lined electric cookers operate on two temperatures. Low is about 200°, or just below boiling, and high is approximately 300°. Besides low temperature, a wrap-around heating system makes this new kind of cooking possible. It eliminates the concentration of heat on the bottom of the pot which causes scorching or requires you to be there to stir occasionally. Believe it or not, hollandaise sauce, which curdles so easily, will hold beautifully at a perfect serving temperature for as long as 6 hours!

Even on high the temperature of the crockery pot cookers is not hot enough for browning. When necessary, it is best to do this in a frying pan. While it does involve another cooking step, it enhances the flavor immeasurably and is well worth the trouble. Always be sure to rinse the frying pan out with a little water, wine or broth and add it to the pot so that none of the delicious flavor and color from the pan drippings is lost.

When cooking meat and chicken there will be a quantity of broth at the finish since there is almost no evaporation during cooking. If there is time, it is possible to reduce the stock by turning the crockery pot temperature to high, but it is considerably faster to ladle the stock into a saucepan and boil it down. The essence you achieve through reducing the stock is far superior to the double quantity of broth you started with.

Crockery pots do have their limitations when it comes to vegetables, especially green ones which loose their beautiful bright color and flavor after hours in the pot. Faster, last minute cooking is better for them.

Not every recipe here uses the crockery pot in its actual preparation. Some use ingredients, such as meat or chicken, which were previously cooked in the crockery pot. "Double cooking" is an excellent way to achieve extra efficiency from your cooker. It pays off in two important ways. It offers economy and a simple way to better utilize your most precious commodity—time!

This international collection of worldly recipes is designed to help you enjoy your crockery pot even more.

SOUPS

Soup has played an important part in the diets of people all over the world. And, no wonder—it is nourishing, inexpensive, easy to prepare, its varieties are endless and all ages can enjoy it. Soup is a natural for crockery pot cooking. The low temperature concept is ideal for capturing the mellow flavor that is only achieved through long, slow cooking. An age-old favorite and one of our newest cooking conveniences make a great combination.

Many of the recipes included here are full meal soups from various parts of the world, all of which are improved by long, slow cooking. Others are first course soups merely heated and kept warm, such as the savory Maritata, which should not be allowed to simmer. A crockery pot serves both purposes well.

Regardless of the kind of soup, the low temperature of a crockery lined cooker makes it ideal for both cooking and serving.

MARITATA

Maritata is a soup for celebrations. In Italy it is the wedding soup. Enjoy it anytime as a rich first course to begin a chicken, veal or fish dinner.

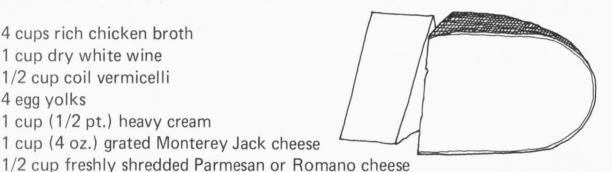

4 cups rich chicken broth
1 cup dry white wine
1/2 cup coil vermicelli
4 egg yolks
1 cup (1/2 pt.) heavy cream
1 cup (4 oz.) grated Monterey Jack cheese
1/2 cup freshly shredded Parmesan or Romano cheese

Heat broth and wine in crockery pot on high (300°). When simmering drop in vermicelli. Cook until al dente, about 10 to 15 minutes. Beat egg yolks until thick and light in color. Beat in cream and cheeses. Ladle a spoonful of hot broth into egg mixture. Then slowly blend into broth in crockery pot. Reduce heat. Heat on low (200°), stirring occasionally, until blended. Makes 6 to 8 first course servings.

VINEYARD CONSOMMÉ

Here is a delightful first course soup to sip in the garden or living room as a prelude to dinner. Serve in small mugs, Japanese tea cups, or small French soufflé dishes.

4 cups rich beef broth*
1 cup dry red wine <u>or</u> dry sherry
salt and pepper to taste
thin lemon or lime slices

Heat broth and wine in crockery pot on high (300°) just until steaming. Season to taste with salt and pepper. Ladle into small mugs. Float a lemon or lime slice in each. Makes 6 to 8 servings.

*canned, homemade, reconstituted beef stock <u>or</u> bouillon cubes

CALDO XOCHITL

6 cups rich chicken stock
1/2 cup vermicelli
3 tbs. vegetable oil
1 whole cooked chicken breast, cut in strips
2 chopped green chiles <u>or</u> 1/4 cup salsa

1 tomato, peeled and chopped
2 green onions, finely chopped
1 avocado
chopped cilantro (Chinese parsley)
toasted pumpkin <u>or</u> sunflower seeds

Heat chicken stock in cockery pot on high (300°). Break vermicelli into 1/2 inch pieces. Using a large frying pan, sauté vermicelli in oil until lightly browned. Drain on paper towels. Add to simmering stock. Cook until al dente, about 10 minutes. Stir in chicken, chiles, tomato and onion. Heat just until hot through. Peel and dice avocado. Place in small bowl. Mound cilantro and seeds in small bowls. Serve condiments alongside soup. Makes about 6 to 8 servings.

MONTEREY CURRY SOUP

Pass this zesty soup in small cups as a prelude to dinner. A crockery pot keeps it hot without over-cooking.

4 tbs. butter	1/2 cup heavy cream
1 tbs. curry powder	2 egg yolks
6 tbs. flour	shredded coconut
2-1/2 cups rich chicken broth	

Melt butter in saucepan. Add curry powder. Cook for several minutes. Stir in flour. Cook 2 to 3 minutes. Stir occasionally. Slowly blend in broth. Continue cooking, stirring constantly, until sauce is thickened. Beat egg yolks. Blend in cream. Stir sauce into egg mixture. Pour into crockery pot. Heat on low (200°) until soup is hot through and thickened. Ladle into cups or bowls. Sprinkle with coconut. Makes 6 first course servings.

KIT CARSON SOUP

This early California soup is claimed to have originated with the famous frontiersman, Kit Carson.

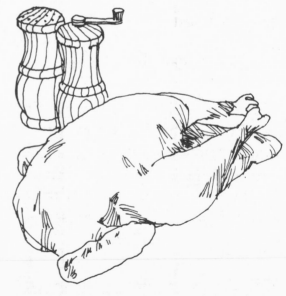

1 (3 lb.) broiler-fryer <u>or</u> 2 turkey drumsticks
1 onion, quartered
1 stalk celery, cut up
1 bay leaf
2 tsp. salt
6 whole black peppercorns
1/2 tsp. Mexican seasoning
1/2 tsp. dried oregano
2 yellow crookneck squash, sliced
1 cup canned chick-peas (garbanzos)
1/4 cup chopped cilantro
3 tbs. salted sunflower <u>or</u> pumpkin seeds
1 avocado, peeled and sliced

Wash chicken (or turkey) well. Place in crockery pot. Add 1 quart water, onion, celery, bay leaf, salt and peppercorns. Cover and cook on low (200°) 8 hours, or until tender. Lift chicken from broth and cool. Remove meat from bones. Cut into 1 inch cubes. Strain stock and return to crockery pot. Turn heat to high (300°). Add Mexican seasoning, oregano, squash and chick-peas. Cover. Cook 1 hour. Add chicken and heat. Ladle into bowls. Sprinkle with cilantro and seeds. Arrange several avocado slices on top of each bowl. Makes 6 servings.

MULLIGATAWNY SOUP

This Indian soup is intended as a full meal. For company dining use choice chicken pieces, such as drumsticks, thighs and breasts exclusively and remove meat from the bones.

1 cup boiling water	3 tbs. butter	2 bay leaves
1 cup shredded coconut	1 tbs. curry powder	chopped cilantro
1 onion, finely chopped	1 broiler-fryer, cut in pieces	hot cooked rice
1 carrot, peeled and grated	4 cups chicken stock	1 lime, cut in wedges

Pour boiling water over coconut and let stand. Using a large frying pan, sauté onion and carrot in butter until limp and golden. Add curry powder. Cook 3 to 4 minutes. Add chicken and sauté until browned. Transfer to crockery pot. Drain coconut through wire strainer. Save liquid. Discard coconut. Add coconut liquid, stock and bay leaf to chicken. Season with salt and pepper. Cover crockery pot. Cook on high (300°) 2 to 3 hours, or until tender. Mound rice in each bowl. Ladle in soup. Accompany with lime wedges. Makes 4 to 6 servings.

BEEF AND VEGETABLE SOUP

A hearty beef and vegetable soup makes a fine winter supper. Serve with grated Parmesan cheese and sour dough French bread. Pears and cheese go well for dessert.

2 tbs. olive oil
3 slices (about 1-1/2 pounds) beef shank
1 onion, and chopped
2 carrots, peeled and chopped
1 stalk celery, chopped

2 qts. beef stock
1 can (16 oz.) stewed tomatoes
salt and pepper to taste
1/2 tsp. dried sweet basil

Heat oil in large frying pan. Brown meat on both sides. Place in crockery pot. Add onion, carrots and celery to frying pan. Sauté until limp. Transfer to crockery pot. Add beef stock, tomatoes, salt, pepper and basil. Cover. Cook on low (200°) 8 to 12 hours. Remove meat and bones from broth. Dice meat and discard bones. Skim fat. Return meat to broth and adjust seasonings. Heat through. Ladle into bowls. Makes 8 to 10 servings.

MEXICAN ALBONDIGAS SOUP

Lime juice and cilantro spark this Mexican meat ball soup. Accompany with hot rolled tortillas and finish off with tropical fruit.

1 lb. lean ground chuck
2 qts. rich chicken stock
3 tbs. flour
1 egg
1 red chile pepper, seeds removed
4 carrots, peeled and grated

1/3 cup chopped cilantro
3 tbs. long-grain rice
1/2 lb. spinach, cut in shreds
1/2 tsp. dried oregano
2 tbs. diced ham
2 limes, cut in wedges

Combine ground meat, 1/3 cup chicken stock, flour and egg. Mix well. Shape into 1 inch balls. Place remaining chicken stock, chile pepper, carrots, cilantro and rice in crockery pot. Heat on high (300°). When broth is simmering, add meat balls. Cover. Cook on high (300°) 30 minutes. Turn to low (200°). Cook 2 to 3 hours. Add spinach, oregano and ham. Heat until steaming. Ladle into bowls. Pass lime wedges. Makes 8 servings.

MOROCCAN MEAT BALL SOUP

Chopped tomatoes freshen this spicy meal-in-one soup.

1/3 cup lentils
1 onion, chopped
1 carrot, peeled and grated
1 stalk celery, chopped
2 tbs. salad oil
3/4 cup tomato sauce
1 tsp. grated fresh ginger root*
1/2 tsp. salt
1/2 tsp. cumin
dash seasoned pepper
1-1/2 qt. rich beef or chicken broth
Meat Balls, page 17
1 large tomato, peeled and chopped
3 tbs. cilantro

16

Place lentils with water to cover in saucepan. Cover pan and bring water to boil. Boil 2 minutes. Remove from heat. Let stand 1 hour. Bring to boil again. Simmer 1 hour or until almost tender. Drain. Using a large frying pan, sauté onion, carrot and celery in oil until glazed. Transfer to crockery pot. Add cooked lentils, tomato sauce, ginger, salt, cumin, pepper and stock. Cover and cook on low (200°) 4 hours, or on high (300°) 2 hours. Prepare meat balls while lentils are cooking. When lentils are done drop meat balls into simmering soup. Cover. Cook on high (300°) 30 minutes to 1 hour. Add tomato and cilantro. Serve steaming hot. Makes 6 servings.

Meat Balls—Mix together 1 pound ground lamb, 1/3 cup stock, 3 tablespoons flour, 1 teaspoon salt, 1 clove minced garlic and 2 tablespoons chopped cilantro. Shape into 3/4 inch balls. Roll in flour. Add to soup as directed.

*or 1/4 teaspoon ground ginger

FRENCH ONION SOUP

The wines mellow and lend a subtle flair to this aromatic French-style onion soup.

4 large yellow onions, thinly sliced
1/4 cup butter
3 cups rich beef stock
1 cup dry white wine
1/4 cup medium dry sherry

1 tsp. Worcestershire sauce
1 clove garlic, minced
4 to 6 slices buttered French bread
1/4 cup grated Romano or Parmesan cheese

Using a large frying pan, slowly sauté onions in butter until limp and glazed. Transfer to crockery pot. Add beef stock, white wine, sherry, Worcestershire and garlic. Cover. Cook on low (200°) 6 to 8 hours. Place French bread on a baking sheet. Sprinkle with cheese. Place under preheated broiler until lightly toasted. To serve, ladle soup into bowls. Float a slice of toasted French bread on top. Makes 4 to 6 servings.

COUNTRY-STYLE BEAN SOUP

A meaty ham bone lends substance to a peasant-style pot of bean soup.

1-1/2 cups small white beans, soaked overnight
1 large onion, finely chopped
2 carrots, peeled and shredded
1 stalk celery, finely chopped
3 tbs. olive oil

2 cloves garlic, minced
1 bay leaf
1 meaty ham bone or ham hock
1 tsp. salt
finely chopped parsley

Cover soaked beans with 4-1/2 cups water. Simmer in saucepan 1-1/2 hours, or until almost tender. Transfer beans and liquid to crockery pot. Using a large frying pan, sauté onion, carrots and celery in oil until limp. Transfer to crockery pot. Add garlic, bay leaf, ham bone, salt and 2 cups water. Cover. Cook on low (200°) 6 to 8 hours. Ladle into soup bowls. Sprinkle with parsley. Makes about 8 servings.

GREEK LENTIL SOUP

Hearty bean and lentil soups native to the Middle East and Central Europe are an ideal choice for crockery pot cooking.

1-1/2 cups dried lentils, pre-soaked and drained
1 medium onion, chopped
1 carrot, peeled and grated
1 stalk celery, chopped
3 tbs. olive oil or salad oil
1 bay leaf

2 cloves garlic, minced
1 tsp. salt
1/2 tsp. oregano
1 beef bouillon cube
1/2 cup tomato sauce
3 tbs. red wine vinegar

Simmer lentils in 4-1/2 cups water 1 hour, or until almost tender. Transfer to crockery pot. Using a large frying pan, sauté onion, carrot and celery in oil until limp and glazed. Turn into crockery pot. Add bay leaf, garlic, salt, oregano, and bouillon cube. Cover. Cook on low (200°) 6 to 8 hours. Add tomato sauce and vinegar. Stir well. Cover. Cook on high (300°) 30 minutes, or until flavors are well blended. Makes 8 servings.

SWEDISH-STYLE PEA SOUP

Carrots contribute a pleasant hue and sweetness when smoothly blended into this pea soup. It makes a nourishing luncheon entree or a warm welcome for famished skiers.

1 cup yellow split peas	2 to 3 carrots, peeled and diced
1 meaty ham hock	1 onion, peeled and diced
2 qts. water	salt and pepper to taste
1/2 tsp. dry mustard	2 tbs. dry sherry (optional)

Soak peas and drain. Place in crockery pot with ham hock, water, mustard, carrots and onion. Cover. Cook on low (200°) 8 to 12 hours, or until peas are tender. Remove ham hock. Dice meat. Place vegetables and pea broth in a blender container. Cover. Blend until smooth. Return soup and diced ham to crockery pot. Add salt, pepper and sherry. Heat until steaming. Makes about 8 servings.

POTAGE MONGOLE

Enrich this classic soup with crab meat or shrimp for a hearty luncheon or supper soup. Without the seafood it makes an intriguing starter for a party dinner.

1/2 tsp. curry powder
1 tsp. butter
1 can (10-3/4 oz.) tomato soup
1 can (11-1/2 oz.) green pea soup
1 can (10-1/2 oz.) consommé

2 cups water
2 tbs. dry sherry
1 cup crab meat <u>or</u> shrimp (optional)
finely chopped parsley

Heat crockery pot to high (300°). Add curry powder and butter. Sauté until glazed. (This removes the "raw" taste from curry powder.) Add tomato soup, pea soup, consommé and water. Cover. Heat on high (300°). Add sherry and crab meat or shrimp, if used. Heat until steaming. Ladle into soup bowls. Sprinkle with parsley. Makes 6 to 8 servings.

CREAM OF CORN SOUP

This smooth vegetable soup is especially good preceding a roast pork, ham, or turkey dinner.

1 can (15 oz.) cream-style corn
2 cups rich chicken stock
1 tbs. <u>each</u> chopped celery and onion
1 tsp. Worcestershire sauce
1/2 tsp. celery salt

2 cups milk
salt and pepper to taste
Garnish: popcorn <u>or</u> whipped cream and
              toasted slivered almonds

Combine corn, chicken stock, celery, onion, Worcestershire and celery salt in crockery pot. Cover. Cook on low (200°) 2 hours. Puree in a blender. Return to crockery pot. Add milk, salt and pepper. Heat until steaming. Ladle into soup bowls. Garnish with popcorn or whipped cream and almonds. Makes about 6 servings.

SALADS

In summertime especially, it makes good sense to use your crockery pot to "double cook." Serve the first meal hot and chill the balance for an entirely different meal another day. For example, poach two chickens at once, or an extra large chunk of salmon or halibut, or prepare a quantity size roast or ham. Slow electric cooking seals in all the natural juices, making the resulting meat or chicken succulent and juicy whether served hot or cold.

Cold chicken, fish or meat makes an enticing second presentation as a full-meal salad—the perfect solution for warm weather dining when sagging appetites need a lift. It also frees the "cook" to pursue summertime activities and still serve nutritious meals.

Get into the habit of cooking for two meals at one time and you'll be saving money as well as time.

SWEDISH SALMON PLATE

Cold poached salmon with a sprightly caper dressing makes a refreshing summer supper.

salad greens
1 lb. cold poached salmon*
1 jar (4 or 6 oz.) marinated artichoke hearts
1/3 lb. raw mushrooms, sliced
3 hard-cooked eggs, sliced
1 cucumber, peeled and sliced
1 cup cherry tomatoes, halved
Caper Dressing, page 27

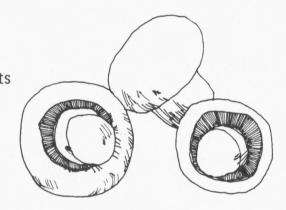

Line a large platter with greens. Place salmon in a chunk in the center. Arrange mounds of drained artichoke hearts, sliced mushrooms, eggs, cucumbers and tomatoes around salmon. Serve buffet style and let each person make their own salad. Pass Caper Dressing. Makes 4 servings.

26

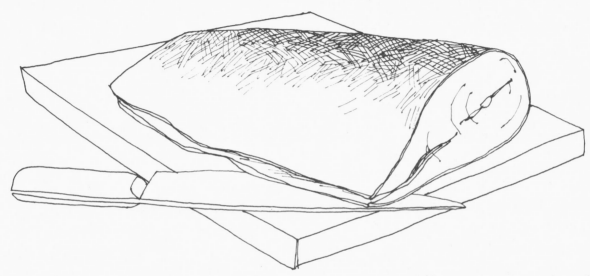

Caper Dressing—Mix together 1/2 cup sour cream, 1/4 cup mayonnaise, 1 teaspoon Dijon-style mustard, 2 tablespoons <u>each</u> parsley and capers, salt and pepper to taste. Makes 1 cup.

*follow directions on page 42

WESTERN COBB SALAD

Pyramid this salad as you assemble it for a striking effect.

1/2 head iceberg lettuce
1/2 bunch endive <u>or</u> romaine lettuce
1/2 bunch watercress
2 cooked chicken breasts, diced*
2 tomatoes, peeled and diced
6 strips crumbled cooked bacon
1 avocado, peeled and diced
2 hard-cooked eggs, shredded
1/2 cup crumbled blue cheese
1 tbs. minced chives
3/4 cup French Dressing, page 29

Finely shred lettuce and endive. Toss in watercress leaves. Arrange in nests on 4 large, chilled plates. Add a layer of chicken. Pile on tomatoes, bacon and avocado. Sprinkle egg and cheese over all. Garnish with chives. Pour dressing on just before serving. If desired, the ingredients may be attractively arranged in a large salad bowl and tossed with the dressing right at the table. Makes 4 generous servings.

French Dressing—Blend together well, 1/2 cup salad oil, 1/4 cup white wine vinegar, 1 minced shallot, salt and pepper to taste. Use as directed.

*poached as directed on page 66

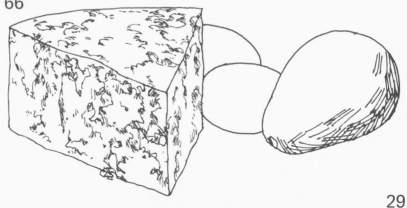

29

CHINESE SHREDDED CHICKEN SALAD

Shop in an oriental market for the specialty ingredients you need for this intriguing tossed chicken salad. There you will find the flat leafed Chinese parsley called cilantro, sesame oil and the translucent noodles labeled rice sticks.

1 large (8 to 10 oz.) chicken breast
1 small head iceberg lettuce, shredded
3 green onions, thinly sliced
1 small bunch cilantro
1 stalk celery, thinly sliced
oil for frying
2 oz. oriental rice sticks
Sesame Oil Dressing, page 31
1/4 cup toasted sesame seeds
1 avocado

Cook chicken as directed for Poached Chicken on page 66. Shred and combine with lettuce, onions, cilantro sprigs and celery in a large salad bowl. Cover and chill while preparing other ingredients. Heat 1/2 inch salad oil in large frying pan. Add a small handful of rice sticks at a time. Fry just until puffed. Lift out with a slotted spoon and drain on paper towels. The noodles fry quickly so it is easier to work with small amounts. When ready to serve salad, add fried noodles to the chilled salad ingredients. Pour on Sesame Oil Dressing. Toss lightly. Sprinkle on sesame seeds. Peel and slice avocado. Arrange in a pinwheel on top. Makes 4 servings.

Sesame Oil Dressing—Mix together in a small container 1 teaspoon salt, 1/2 teaspoon each monosodium glutamate and black pepper, 3 tablespoons white wine vinegar, 2 tablespoons sugar, 1/4 cup salad oil and 1-1/2 tablespoons sesame oil. Makes about 1/2 cup dressing.

INDIAN CHICKEN SALAD BOATS

2-1/2 cups diced cooked chicken*
1/2 cup sliced celery
3/4 cup Thompson seedless grapes
Chutney Salad Dressing

2 small cantaloupes, halved and seeded
3 tbs. toasted slivered almonds or
    chopped macadamia nuts

Toss diced chicken, celery, grapes, and Chutney Salad Dressing together in a bowl. Spoon a mound of salad mixture into each cantaloupe half shell. Sprinkle with nuts. Place on salad plates. If desired, scoop melon into balls. Mix melon balls into the chicken salad then serve in scooped out shells. Makes 4 servings.

Chutney Salad Dressing—Place 1/3 cup sour cream, 3 tablespoons mayonnaise, 1/4 cup (or more) Major Grey's chutney, 1/2 teaspoon lemon peel, and 1 tablespoon lemon juice in blender container. Cover. Blend just until smooth. Use as directed.

*poached as directed on page 66

32

BEEF AND MUSHROOMS VINAIGRETTE

Slices of beef leftover from Sauerbrauten, Beef a la Mode or a pot roast make a great second appearance in this hearty salad.

1 jar (6 oz.) marinated artichoke hearts
1/4 cup safflower oil
2 tbs. _each_ lemon juice and white wine vinegar
1/4 cup dry white wine _or_ Vermouth
2 green onions, finely chopped
1/4 tsp. _each_ salt and tarragon
freshly ground pepper

1/2 lb. mushrooms, thinly sliced
1-1/2 lb. leftover beef roast, sliced
1 cup cherry tomatoes, halved
1/2 cup pitted ripe olives _or_
    small gerkins
2 tbs. finely chopped parsley _or_
    chives

Drain marinade from artichoke hearts into a bowl. Mix in oil, lemon juice, vinegar, wine, onions, salt, tarragon and pepper. Add mushrooms and cut-up artichoke hearts. Mix to coat thoroughly. Cover and chill 1 hour. Arrange sliced beef in a shallow serving dish. Spoon vegetables and marinade over beef slices. Ring platter with tomatoes and olives. Sprinkle with parsley. Makes 4 to 6 servings.

33

SUMMER RUSSIAN SALAD

This assorted meat salad is a handsome way to reintroduce leftover roast. Accompany with dark Russian rye bread and dill pickles.

1/2 lb. <u>each</u> cooked roast beef and ham <u>or</u> roast lamb
1/2 lb. <u>each</u> Italian salami and Mortadella
1 small red onion, finely chopped
1/3 cup finely chopped parsley
1/4 cup capers
Homemade Mayonnaise, page 35
endive <u>or</u> romaine leaves
cherry tomatoes
hard-cooked eggs for garnish

Slice leftover roasts. Cut into matchstick pieces. Slice cold cuts into julienne strips. Place in large bowl. Add onion, parsley and capers. Mix in enough mayonnaise to bind. Spoon onto serving platter lined with greens. Ring with cherry tomatoes and 2 or 3 hard-cooked eggs, quartered. Makes 6 to 8 servings.

Homemade Mayonnaise—Place 1 egg, 1-1/2 tablespoons <u>each</u> lemon juice and white wine vinegar, 1 teaspoon Dijon-style mustard, 1/2 teaspoon <u>each</u> salt and sugar in blender container. Blend a few seconds. With motor running, gradually pour in 7/8 cup (1 cup minus 2 tablespoons) safflower oil in a slow steady stream. When all oil has been used and mixture has thickened, turn out into a refrigerator jar. Cover and chill. Makes about 1 cup.

CURRIED HAM AND GRAPE SALAD

Other leftover roast meats such as veal, turkey or lamb are surprisingly good substitutes for ham in this cool combination.

1 lb. cooked ham
1-1/2 cups seedless grapes
1 small cucumber, peeled and diced
2 stalks celery, chopped
1 small avocado, peeled and diced
1/4 cup <u>each</u> mayonnaise and sour cream
1 tsp. <u>each</u> curry powder and honey
1 small head romaine

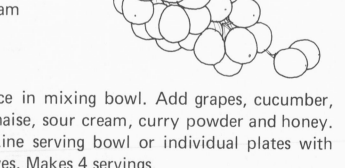

Cut ham into julienne strips. Place in mixing bowl. Add grapes, cucumber, celery and avocado. Combine mayonnaise, sour cream, curry powder and honey. Mix lightly with salad ingredients. Line serving bowl or individual plates with romaine. Spoon salad onto lettuce leaves. Makes 4 servings.

GATE HOUSE SALAD

Piquant blue cheese dressing makes a rich topping for this handsome salad.

1/4 lb. <u>each</u> Swiss and Canadian cheddar cheese
1/2 lb. cooked ham
1/2 lb. roast beef <u>or</u> chicken breast
iceberg lettuce
cherry tomatoes

garbanzo beans
1 small green pepper,
   thinly sliced
Gate House Dressing

Cut cheese and meats into julienne strips. Line large individual salad bowls or plates with lettuce leaves. Arrange mounds of cheese, ham and roast beef or chicken on lettuce. Garnish with cherry tomatoes, beans and pepper rings. Pass dressing. Makes 4 servings.

Gate House Dressing—Place 1 cup sour cream, 1/2 teaspoon <u>each</u> garlic salt and sugar, freshly ground pepper to taste, 1-1/2 tablespoons lemon juice and 2 ounces blue cheese in blender container. Blend until smooth. Turn into a sauce bowl. Crumble an additional 1 ounce blue cheese over the top. Makes 1-1/4 cups.

CAESAR SALAD SUPREME

Sliced cold meats transform the classic Caesar Salad into a full meal.

2 slices sour dough French bread
2 tbs. butter
1 clove garlic, minced
1 large head romaine
1/3 cup olive or safflower oil
2 tbs. white wine vinegar
1/2 tsp. each salt and Dijon-style mustard
6 anchovy fillets, chopped
1 egg
juice of 1/2 lemon
3/4 lb. assorted sliced meats: salami, smoked tongue, corned beef, ham
1 jar (4 oz.) artichoke hearts
1/2 cup shredded Parmesan cheese
freshly ground pepper

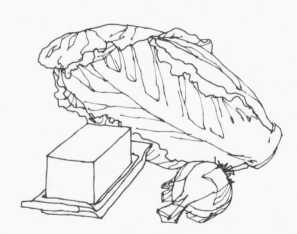

38

Cut bread into cubes. Sauté in butter with garlic until golden brown. Drain on paper towels. Tear greens into bite-size pieces. Put in salad bowl. Shake oil, vinegar, salt, mustard and anchovies together in jar. Place egg in a small pan of simmering water. Remove from heat and let stand 1 minute. Toss dressing and lettuce together. Add coddled egg. Toss until coated. Sprinkle with lemon juice. Mix again. Add meat, croutons, artichoke hearts and cheese. Toss. Sprinkle with freshly ground pepper. Makes 4 servings.

FISH

Fish is delicate and should always be prepared with care and gentleness. It demands more precise watching and timing than most foods being cooked in a crockery pot. If overcooked it looses its juicy tenderness. The low temperature setting of crockery-lined, slow cookers is perfect for fish. But, unlike meat, extra long cooking is destined to shrink the delicate fibers and make the flesh tough. In timing, be sure to allow for variables which will occur with different shaped pieces of fish. Feel free to test for doneness before the specified time is up. When fish is done, it will flake easily when tested with a fork but still be moist. It should be removed from the pot as soon as it is done.

POACHED SALMON

Poach a large piece of salmon for two meals. Serve part of it warm with Cilantro Butter. Mask the remainder in wine aspic for its second showing.

2 lb. (or larger) piece salmon
1/2 cup dry white wine
1/2 cup water
1 bay leaf
few celery leaves
1 green onion
1/2 tsp. salt
1 tbs. lemon juice
1/2 lemon, thinly sliced
Cilantro Butter, page 43

Place salmon in crockery pot. Pour in wine and water. Add bay leaf, celery leaves, onion, salt and lemon juice. Lay lemon slices on top of salmon. Cover and cook on low (200°) 2 to 3 hours, or until salmon flakes when tested with a fork. Remove salmon from crockery pot. Strain poaching juices into a refrigerator jar. Cover and chill until needed for aspic. Remove skin and bones from salmon. Cut half of salmon into serving pieces. Serve warm with Cilantro Butter. Makes 3 to 4 servings. Prepare Salmon In Aspic, page 44, with remaining half of fish.

Cilantro Butter—Heat 1/4 cup butter, 3 tablespoons lemon juice, 1 finely chopped shallot or green onion and 3 tablespoons finely chopped cilantro leaves in saucepan. Serve with Poached Salmon.

SALMON IN ASPIC

Poached salmon in jellied aspic makes a handsome, French-style first course. Or if you prefer, serve it as an entree salad, garnished with cherry tomatoes, marinated artichoke hearts and crisp cucumber spears.

1 cup poaching juices (page 42)
1/2 cup dry white wine
1-1/2 tsp. unflavored gelatine
1/2 cup water
3 doz. large capers
1 lb. poached salmon
1/2 cup Homemade Mayonnaise, page 35

Remove any solidified fat from the top of jellied poaching juices saved as directed on page 42. Heat juices and wine until steaming. Soften gelatine in cold water. Add to hot mixture. Remove from heat. Stir until gelatine is dissolved. Pour a layer of aspic into 6 small molds or custard cups. (Set remaining aspic mixture aside. Do not chill.) Place 6 capers in each mold. Chill. When set, lay pieces of salmon, bones and skin removed, on each jellied layer. Pour in remaining aspic to cover. Chill until set. To serve, quickly dip molds into warm water and turn out onto plates. Garnish with Homemade Mayonnaise. Makes 6 servings.

BAKED FISH, PLAKA STYLE

Fish fillets are smothered in vegetables for this flavorful Grecian dish.

4 medium onions, thinly sliced
3 tbs. olive oil
2 tomatoes
1/4 cup finely chopped parsley
2 cloves garlic, minced

1-1/3 lbs. turbot or sole fillets
2 tbs. lemon juice
salt and pepper to taste
1 lemon, thinly sliced

Using a large frying pan, slowly sauté onions in oil until golden brown and almost caramelized. Peel and chop 1 tomato. Add to onions, along with parsley and garlic. Simmer a few minutes longer. Place fish fillets in a lightly buttered crockery pot. Sprinkle with lemon juice, salt and pepper. Spoon sautéed vegetables over fish. Slice remaining tomato and place on vegetables. Top with lemon slices. Cover crockery pot. Cook on low (200°) for about 1-1/2 hours, or until fish flakes with a fork. Makes 4 servings.

TURBOT IN A CLOAK

The zest of citrus peel permeates fish fillets as they bake to tenderness in this low calorie entree.

1-1/3 lbs. turbot fillets
salt and pepper
3 green onions, finely chopped
1 tbs. olive oil
1/2 cup finely chopped parsley
1 tsp. <u>each</u> grated lemon peel and orange peel
1 orange, thinly sliced

Place fish fillets in buttered crockery pot. Sprinkle with salt and pepper. Toss green onions in oil just to coat. Stir in parsley and citrus peels. Sprinkle over fish. Cover. Cook on low (200°) about 1-1/2 hours, or until fish flakes when tested with a fork. Transfer to serving platter and arrange an orange slice on top of each fillet. Makes 4 servings.

FISH FILLETS PAPRIKA STYLE

Sour cream and paprika add a nice Hungarian touch to this fish entree.

1-1/3 lbs. sole, turbot, <u>or</u>
    other white fish fillets
salt and pepper
2/3 cup sour cream
2 tsp. flour
3 green onions, finely chopped

3 tbs. dry white wine
1/2 tsp. paprika
    (imported Hungarian style, preferred)
chopped parsley
lemon wedges

Season fish fillets with salt and pepper. Place in buttered crockery pot. Mix together sour cream, flour, onions and wine. Spoon over fish. Sprinkle with paprika. Cover. Cook on low (200°) about 1-1/2 hours, or until fish flakes when tested with a fork. Garnish each serving with parsley and lemon wedges. Makes 4 servings.

SHRIMP-STUFFED SOLE ROLLS

Fish rolls bask in a sherried sauce as they poach to tenderness.

6 (about 1-1/2 lbs.) sole fillets
salt and pepper
2 tbs. butter
1/2 lb. small cooked shrimp*
1 can (10-1/2 oz.) cream of mushroom soup, undiluted

1/3 cup pale dry sherry
2 tbs. lemon juice
1/4 cup grated Parmesan cheese

Season each fish fillet with salt and pepper. Dot with 1 teaspoon butter. Spoon about 2 tablespoons shrimp in the center of each fillet and roll up. Skewer with a toothpick. Place in buttered crockery pot. Combine soup, sherry and lemon juice in saucepan. Heat, stirring until blended. Pour over fish. Sprinkle with cheese and dust lightly with paprika. Cover and cook on low (200°) about 1-1/2 hours, or until fish flakes when tested. Garnish with parsley. Makes 6 servings.

*or 1 can (6-1/2 oz.) shrimp, drained

SCALLOPS IN WINE

Scallops and mushrooms braise together for a succulent sauce to spoon over pilaff.

1/4 cup butter
1/4 cup dry white wine
2 tbs. minced parsley
1 tbs. chopped shallots or green onions
2 tbs. pale dry sherry
1 lb. scallops
1/2 lb. mushrooms, thinly sliced

Combine butter, wine, parsley, shallots and sherry in crockery pot. Cook, uncovered, on high (300°) until sauce bubbles and is reduced slightly. Add scallops and mushrooms. Cover. Cook 10 to 15 minutes, or until cooked through. Makes 4 servings.

CIOPPINO GENOVESE

In this fun-to-eat fish stew, the shrimp, crab and clams are cooked right in the sauce with their shells still on, so each person must remove his own. Small terry cloth towels make perfect napkins for this meal.

1 onion, finely chopped
1/4 cup olive oil
2 cloves garlic, minced
2 tbs. chopped parsley
1 can (16 oz.) tomatoes
1 can (8 oz.) tomato sauce
salt and pepper to taste

1 tbs. freshly chopped basil*
1/2 cup pale dry sherry
1 bottle (8 oz.) clam juice
1 lb. rock cod or halibut
1 doz. or more fresh clams
12 fresh shrimp
1 fresh cracked crab, uncooked

Using a large frying pan, sauté onion in oil until glazed. Add garlic and parsley. Sauté a few minutes. Turn into crockery pot. Add tomatoes, tomato sauce, salt, pepper, basil, sherry and clam juice. Cover and cook on low (200°) 2 hours or on high (300°) 1 hour. Cut fish in two inch cubes. Add fish cubes, clams,

52

shrimp and crab to sauce. Cover. Cook on high (300°) 30 minutes or until shrimp turn pink, clams open and fish flakes when tested with a fork. Ladle into large soup bowls. Makes 6 servings.

*or Pesto Sauce or 3/4 teaspoon dried basil

POULTRY

Chicken cooked in a crockery-lined, slow electric cooker is remarkably succulent. Moist, plump poached chicken is one of the crockery pot's finest accomplishments. It is superior to other methods of poaching. Since the variety of chicken dishes is endless, and because chicken is plentiful, popular and economical, the recipes which follow all call for chicken. However, other kinds of poultry such as turkey parts, game hens and even rabbit, may be used. Included in this collection of recipes are some all-time favorites along with a few unusual ones which perhaps will become favorites.

STUFFED ROAST CHICKEN

A plump stuffed chicken is an ideal choice to roast in a large 4-1/2-quart size crockery pot. If yours is smaller, stand the bird breast down, legs up.

3 lb. broiler-fryer
1 pkg. (6 oz.) white and wild rice almondine
1 tbs. butter
salt and pepper

1/2 tsp. grated lemon peel
1/4 cup golden raisins
1/2 cup dry white wine

Thoroughly wash chicken. Pat dry. Cook rice almondine according to package directions. Using a large frying pan, brown chicken in butter. Turn to brown on all sides. Season well with salt and pepper. Sprinkle lemon peel inside the cavity. Mix raisins into rice mixture. Spoon into cavity. Skewer opening closed. Place chicken in crockery pot. Pour in wine. Cover and cook on low (200°) 7 to 8 hours or until tender. Transfer to a carving board. Skim fat from pan drippings. Pour juices into a sauce bowl. Carve bird. Serve at once. Makes about 6 servings.

LEMON ROAST CHICKEN

Greek cooks season roast chicken in a simple fashion—rubbed with garlic, oregano and lemon juice. The result is succulent and aromatic.

1 (3 lb. or larger) broiler-fryer
salt and pepper
1 tsp. crumbled, dried oregano
2 cloves garlic, minced

2 tbs. butter
1/4 cup water
3 tbs. lemon juice

Wash chicken and giblets. Pat dry. Season chicken with salt and pepper. Sprinkle half the oregano and garlic inside cavity. Melt butter in a large frying pan. Brown chicken on all sides. Transfer to crockery pot. Sprinkle with remaining oregano and garlic. Add water to frying pan. Stir to loosen brown bits. Pour into crockery pot. Cover. Cook on low (200°) 8 hours. Add lemon juice the last hour of cooking. Transfer chicken to carving board. Skim fat and pour juices into a sauce bowl. Carve bird. Serve with some of juices spooned over chicken. Makes 6 servings.

COQ AU VIN

Chicken takes on a rich smoky flavor and tang of wine in this classic entree.

3 green onions
3 slices bacon, diced
1 (about 3 lbs.) broiler-fryer
1 tsp. salt
1/2 tsp. dried thyme
8 small whole onions
2 cups dry red wine
2 tsp. chicken stock base*
1 clove garlic, minced
1/2 lb. mushrooms
2 tbs. butter
1-1/2 tbs. cornstarch
2 tbs. cold water

Chop white part of onions only. Sauté bacon and chopped onion in large frying pan until bacon is crisp. Transfer to crockery pot. Wash chicken. Pat dry with paper towels. Add to bacon drippings. Season with salt and thyme. Brown on all sides. Transfer to crockery pot. Peel whole onions. Cut a small cross in the root end of each. Brown in remaining drippings. Add to crockery pot. Pour wine into frying pan. Stir to loosen brown bits. Add chicken stock base. Stir until dissolved. Pour over chicken. Add garlic. Cover. Cook on low (200°) 6 to 8 hours. Slice mushrooms. Sauté in butter. Add to chicken. Turn heat to high (300°). When juices bubble, stir in cornstarch and water which have been blended together. Cook until thickened. Serve sprinkled with parsley. Makes 4 to 6 servings.

*or 2 bouillon cubes

HAWAIIAN CHICKEN

Browned pineapple slices and buttery avocado spears complement golden chicken breasts.

4 green onions
3 to 4 tbs. butter
4 chicken breast halves
flour seasoned with salt and pepper

1 flat can (14-1/4 oz.) sliced pineapple
1 avocado, peeled
hot buttered rice

Chop onions using only 1 inch of green tops. Sauté in 1 tablespoon of butter until glazed. Transfer to crockery pot. Coat chicken breasts in seasoned flour. Sauté in butter until brown on both sides. Transfer to crockery pot. Drain pineapple. Pour juice over chicken. Cover. Cook on low (200°) 3 to 4 hours (high (300°) 1-1/2 to 2 hours) or until breasts are tender. Sauté pineapple slices in butter until golden. Place on heated platter. Top each with a chicken breast. Slice avocado into 8 lengthwise strips. Place 2 strips on each chicken breast. Serve pan drippings over rice. Makes 4 servings.

CHICKEN, MUSHROOM AND ARTICHOKE CASSEROLE

1 (about 3 lbs.) broiler-fryer
1 tsp. salt
freshly ground pepper
1/2 tsp. paprika
3 tbs. butter
1/2 cup rich chicken broth

3 tbs. dry sherry
1 tsp. fresh tarragon (1/4 tsp. dried)
1/4 lb. mushrooms, sliced
1 tbs. cornstarch
1 can (15 oz.) artichoke hearts, drained

Wash chicken. Pat dry with paper towels. Season with salt, pepper and paprika. Using a large frying pan, brown chicken in 1 tablespoon butter. Transfer to crockery pot. Pour broth and sherry into pan. Stir to loosen brown bits. Pour over chicken. Season with tarragon. Cover. Cook on low (200°) 8 hours. Just before serving, sauté mushrooms in remaining butter until glazed. Combine cornstarch with an equal amount of cold water. Turn crockery pot to high (300°). When sauce is simmering, stir in cornstarch mixture. Cook until thickened. Add sautéed mushrooms and artichoke hearts. Heat and serve. Makes 6 servings.

CHICKEN WITH CALVADOS

The Normandy section of France is noted for this succulent chicken entree. It calls for apple brandy, a specialty of the region.

1 large broiler-fryer*
2 tbs. butter
1 tsp. salt
1/4 cup Calvados (apple brandy)
1 tbs. chicken stock base
2 tbs. chopped parsley
1/2 tsp. mixed dried marjoram, tarragon and thyme
1/2 cup dry white wine
1 tbs. arrowroot
2 tbs. water
1/4 cup heavy cream

Wash chicken. Cut into serving pieces. Pat dry with paper towel. Using a large frying pan, sauté chicken in butter until nicely browned. Season with salt. Pour Calvados over chicken. Carefully ignite. Use a long wooden match if available. Spoon pan juices over chicken while flaming. Remove chicken and pan juices to crockery pot. Combine chicken stock base, parsley, herbs and wine. Pour over chicken. Cover. Cook on low (200°) 6 to 8 hours. Remove chicken to heated platter. Turn heat to high (300°). Blend arrowroot with water. Stir into pan juices. Cook on high until mixture thickens and boils. Stir in cream. Heat to serving temperature. Makes 4 to 6 servings.

*or 4 breast halves and 4 thighs

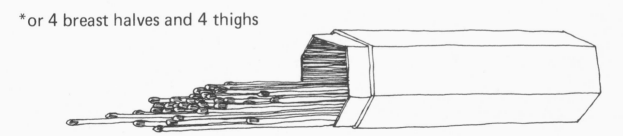

 **CHICKEN PROVENCAL**

This country-style chicken entree intertwines the influence of Spanish, French and Italian cuisines. Rice pilaff or rissoto makes a good side dish.

1 (about 3 lbs.) broiler-fryer, cut in pieces
3 slices bacon, diced
2 tbs. <u>each</u> butter and oil
1 carrot, peeled and grated
4 shallots, chopped
3 tbs. brandy <u>or</u> Cognac

2 tomatoes, peeled and chopped
2/3 cup dry red wine
1/4 tsp. <u>each</u> marjoram, tarragon
    and basil
salt and pepper to taste

Wash chicken pieces. Pat dry with paper towels. Using a large frying pan, brown bacon until crisp. Remove from pan. Pour off drippings. Add butter and oil to frying pan. Sauté carrot and shallots until limp. Push to sides of pan. Add chicken pieces and sauté until brown. Pour in brandy and ignite. When flames die, transfer chicken and vegetables to crockery pot. Add tomatoes, wine, herbs, bacon, salt and pepper. Cover. Cook on low (200°) 8 hours. Remove cover. Skim off fat. Cook juices down until reduced by half. Makes 6 servings.

POACHED CHICKEN

Chicken poached in a crockery pot is the best ever. Whenever possible poach an extra one to use in cool supper salads, lovely crêpes, enchiladas and other casseroles. The following is the basic poaching method. Cooking time will be the same even when the recipe is doubled. A 4-1/2 quart crockery pot will accommodate two whole 3-pound chickens nicely.

1 (about 3 lbs.) broiler-fryer
salt and pepper
2-inch piece celery
1 carrot
1/2 onion
1 cup chicken broth
1 bay leaf

Wash chicken and giblets. Pat dry with paper towels. Place in crockery pot. Season with salt and pepper. Tuck celery, carrot and onion around chicken. Pour

66

in broth. Add bay leaf. Cover. Cook on low (200°) 7 to 8 hours, or until chicken is tender. Lift chicken from pot. Let stand until cool enough to handle. Strain stock into refrigerator container. Chill. Lift off fat. Remove chicken meat from bones in as large pieces as possible. Place in a container. Cover and chill. Use in salads or casserole dishes. Yields about 2-1/2 to 3 cups chicken meat and 1 cup jellied stock.

POACHED CHICKEN VERONIQUE

Seedless grapes add a special flavor to chicken. If you prefer, use chicken parts instead of a whole bird. Cooking time will be shortened by about 1 hour.

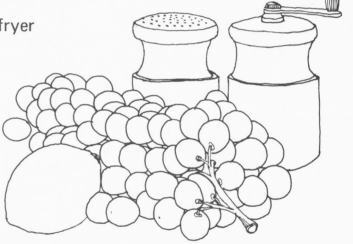

1 large (3 to 3-1/2 lbs.) whole broiler-fryer
1 tbs. butter
1 small carrot, peeled and chopped
1 small onion, peeled and chopped
1/2 cup dry white wine
1/2 cup chicken broth
salt and pepper to taste
3 tbs. orange marmalade
1 tbs. lemon juice
1-1/2 cups Thompson seedless grapes

Wash chicken and giblets. Pat dry with paper towels. Using a large frying pan, brown chicken and giblets in butter. Add carrot and onion. Sauté until glazed.

68

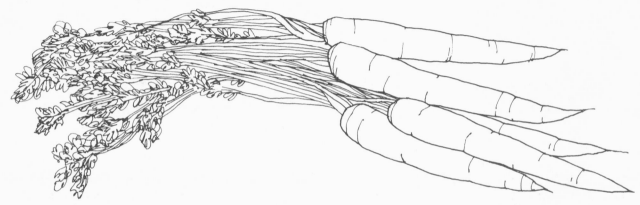

Transfer chicken, giblets and vegetables to crockery pot. Pour wine and broth into frying pan. Stir to loosen brown bits. Pour over chicken. Season with salt and pepper. Cover. Cook on low (200°) 7 to 8 hours, or until tender. Transfer chicken and giblets to heated platter and keep warm. Strain pan juices into saucepan. Discard cooking vegetables. Skim fat from pan juices. Bring to boil. Cook down until reduced to 1 cup. Add marmalade, lemon juice and grapes. Heat to serving temperature. Serve in a sauce bowl. Pass with chicken. Makes 6 servings.

POACHED CHICKEN IN TARRAGON WINE SAUCE

An herb-flavored wine sauce gilds this roasted bird.

1 (3 to 3-1/2 lb.) broiler-fryer	1 tbs. butter	1 cup chicken stock
1 carrot, peeled and chopped	1 bay leaf	1 tsp. tarragon
1 onion, peeled and chopped	1 cup dry white wine	salt and pepper

Wash fryer. Pat dry with paper towels. Sauté carrot and onion in butter in a large frying pan. Transfer vegetables to crockery pot. Brown fryer in remaining drippings. Transfer to crockery pot. Add bay leaf, wine, stock, tarragon, salt and pepper. Cover. Cook on low (200°) 8 hours. Remove chicken from crockery pot. Keep warm. Pour juices into saucepan. Skim fat. Boil down until reduced to 1 cup. Pour into sauce bowl. Carve chicken. Serve on warm platter. Pass sauce. Makes 4 to 6 serings.

Variation—Beat 2 egg yolks with 1/3 cup heavy cream. Stir part of reduced sauce into cream mixture. Return mixture to saucepan. Cook, stirring, until thickened. Pass with chicken. Makes 4 to 6 servings.

CHICKEN IN ORANGE SAUCE

Orange juice concentrate and currant jelly make a piquant, delicious sauce.

1 (3 to 3-1/2 lb.) broiler-fryer, cut-up
1 tbs. butter
1 carrot, peeled and chopped
1 green onion, chopped
1 cup chicken stock

salt and pepper
1/4 cup undiluted orange juice concentrate
1/4 cup currant jelly
1 orange, peeled and cut in segments
1 bunch watercress (optional)

Wash chicken. Pat dry with paper towels. Using a large frying pan, brown chicken in butter. Add carrot and onion. Sauté until glazed. Transfer chicken and vegetables to crockery pot. Pour stock into pan. Stir to loosen brown bits. Pour over chicken. Sprinkle with salt and pepper. Cover. Cook on low (200°) 6 to 8 hours. Remove chicken from pot and keep warm. Strain pan juices into saucepan. Skim fat. Reduce to 1 cup. Add orange juice concentrate and currant jelly. Heat until blended. Spoon some of sauce over chicken. Garnish with orange segments and watercress sprigs. Pass remaining sauce. Makes 6 servings.

CHICKEN IN THE POT

Cook pan juices down to gain a rich, thick sauce for the chicken.

1 (3-1/2 lb.) whole broiler-fryer
salt and pepper
1 tbs. butter
2 carrots, sliced diagonally
2 parsnips, cut in strips
2 stalks celery, cut in 1-inch pieces
1 leek or 3 green onions, sliced
2 cloves garlic, minced
1/2 tsp. dried oregano
2 cups chicken broth
1 cup dry white wine

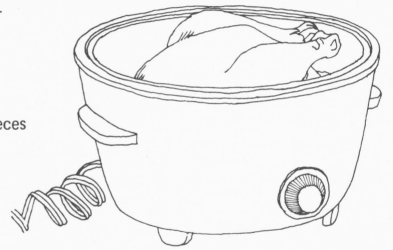

Wash chicken and giblets. Pat dry with paper towels. Season with salt and pepper. Using a large frying pan, brown chicken and giblets in butter. Transfer to crockery pot. Rinse out drippings with water. Pour into crockery pot. Place carrots, parsnips, celery and leek around chicken. Season vegetables with salt and pepper. Add garlic, oregano, broth and wine. Cover pot. Cook on low (200°) 8 hours, or until tender. Remove chicken and vegetables to a platter. Keep warm. Pour pan juices into a saucepan. Skim fat. Boil down until reduced to 1 cup. Makes 6 servings.

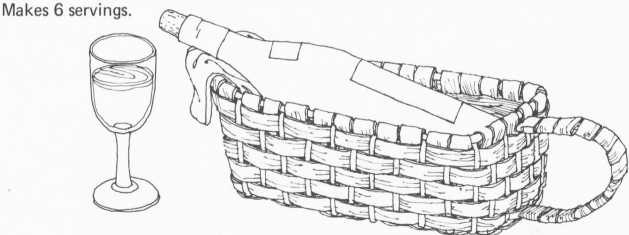

CHICKEN AND CHERRIES JUBILEE

For a dramatic party dish, flame chicken and cherries at the table.

2 (2-1/2 to 3 lbs. each) broiler-fryers*
2 tbs. butter
salt and pepper
1 can (1 lb.) pitted Bing cherries
1/2 cup chili sauce
2 chicken bouillon cubes**
1/4 cup pale dry sherry
2 tbs. cornstarch
2 tbs. water
3 tbs. brandy or Cognac, warmed

Wash chicken. Pat dry with paper towels. Melt butter in a large frying pan. Brown chicken on all sides. Transfer to crockery pot. Season with salt and pepper. Pour 1/2 cup cherry juice into frying pan. Stir to loosen drippings. Pour over chicken. Add chili sauce and bouillon cubes. Cover. Cook on low (200°) 6 to 8 hours, or until tender. Remove chicken from pot and keep warm. Pour pan juices into saucepan. Skim fat. Boil down until slightly reduced. Add sherry and remaining cherry juice. Combine cornstarch and water. Stir into juice mixture. Cook until thickened. Add cherries and heat. Arrange chicken on warm platter. Ignite warmed brandy and flame sauce. Spoon flaming sauce over chicken. Makes 10 to 12 servings.

*or breasts, thighs and drumsticks only
**or 2 teaspoons chicken stock base

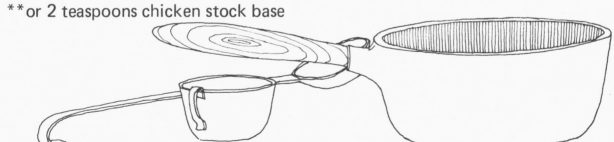

CHICKEN CURRY

This is a good dish to prepare in stages. Cook the chicken one day and finish it in the sauce the next. Apple chunks add tang and texture to the sauce.

1 (2-1/2 to 3 lbs.) whole broiler-fryer
2 cups water
3 chicken bouillon cubes*
1 large tart cooking apple
1/4 cup butter
1 large onion, finely chopped
3 stalks celery, thinly sliced
1 tbs. curry powder
salt to taste
dash red pepper
hot steamed rice
Condiments, page 77

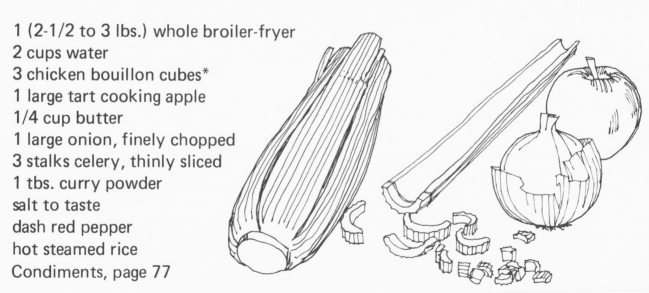

Place chicken in crockery pot with water and bouillon. Cover. Cook on low (200°) 7 to 8 hours (high (300°) 3 to 4 hours) or until tender. Remove from broth. Cool. Remove chicken from bones. Dice. Peel, core and dice apple. Sauté in butter with onion, celery and curry powder until limp and glazed. Season with salt and pepper. Transfer to crockery pot. Add diced chicken and enough broth to moisten. Cook on low (200°) until hot. Serve over rice. Pass condiments. Makes 6 to 8 servings.

Condiments: toasted slivered almonds, chutney, crisp bacon, toasted coconut and golden raisins.

*or 1 tbs. chicken stock base

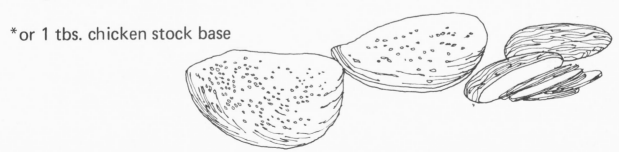

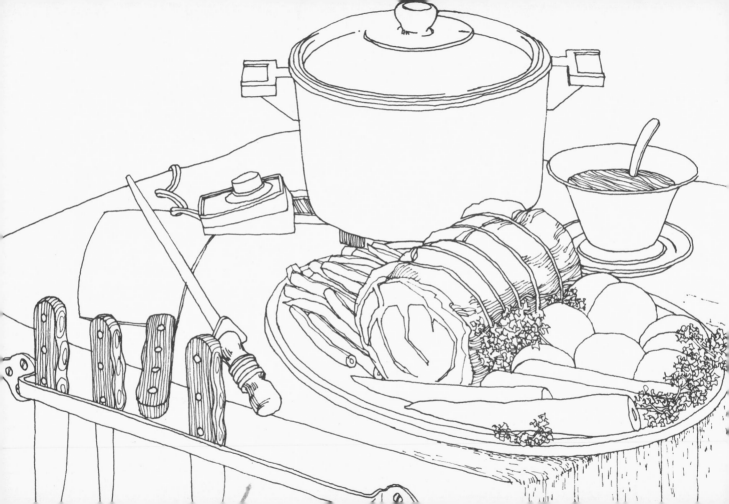

MEATS AND CASSEROLES

Meats are the real stars of "crockery potting." The long slow cooking at a low temperature results in truly juicy cuts with almost no shrinkage. Most often these are the less expensive cuts which adds still more to the economy of slow electric cooking, the crockery pot way.

Another greatly appreciated feature of cooking by this method is the ease with which meat can be kept at a perfect serving temperature without overcooking it.

The offering here is a collection of international dishes such as French beef stews, German pot roasts, Mediterranean meat sauces, Indian curries, Morrocan tajines, Mexican casseroles, sausages in wine, fruited pork chops and country-style pates. All are easily and perfectly prepared this convenient way.

SAUERBRAUTEN

In order for the meat to acquire the distinguishing piquancy of this classic German dish it should be marinated at least three days.

4 to 5 pound beef rump roast
Marinade, page 81
2 tbs. bacon drippings or oil
1 onion, chopped
1 cup beef stock
2 tbs. cornstarch
2 tbs. cold water

Place meat in a deep bowl. Add marinade. Cover and refrigerate at least 3 days. Turn occasionally. When ready to cook, remove meat from marinade. Pat dry with paper towels. Strain marinade and set aside. Heat drippings in a large frying pan. Brown meat on all sides. Add onions. Sauté until golden. Transfer meat and onions to crockery pot. Add stock and 1 cup strained marinade. Cover.

Cook on low (200°) 8 to 10 hours or until tender. Remove to heated platter and keep warm. Turn heat to high (300°). Blend cornstarch and water. When gravy is bubbling, stir in cornstarch mixture. Cook until thickened. Serve with meat. Makes 12 to 14 servings.

Marinade—Combine 1-1/2 cups dry red wine, 3/4 cup red wine vinegar, 1 cup water, 1 <u>each</u> carrot and onion, peeled and chopped, 1 bay leaf, 10 whole peppercorns, 6 whole colves, 1/2 tsp. thyme and 1 tsp. salt in a large saucepan. Bring to a boil. Simmer 5 minutes. Remove from heat. Cool and use as directed.

BEEF A LA MODE

This renowned French pot roast achieves supremacy when slowly cooked in a crockery pot.

Marinade, page 83
4 lb. beef rump roast
1 tbs. butter
2 beef bouillon cubes
1/4 cup tomato sauce
chopped parsley

Place roast in large bowl with marinade. Cover. Chill 1 day. Turn occasionally. To cook, remove meat from marinade. Pat dry with paper towels. Melt butter in a large frying pan. Brown meat on all sides. Place in crockery pot. Strain marinade reserving vegetables. Add marinade to meat. Sauté vegetables in frying pan until glazed. Add to meat. Loosen pan drippings with a little water. Add to crockery pot along with bouillon and tomato sauce. Cover. Cook on low (200°) 8 hours, or

until meat is tender. Transfer meat to carving board. Pour juices into saucepan. Boil until reduced to 2 cups. Serve in a sauce bowl. Garnish with parsley. Makes about 10 servings.

Marinade—Combine 1-1/2 teaspoon salt, 1 teaspoon dried thyme, freshly ground pepper, 1 <u>each</u> carrot, celery stalk and onion, peeled and chopped, 2 cloves garlic, minced and 2 cups dry red wine in a large bowl. Use as directed.

POT ROAST PACIFIC

Teriyaki seasonings richly flavor and glaze this chuck roast.

4 to 5 lb. chuck roast	1 tbs. chopped fresh ginger _or_ 1-1/2 tsp. ground ginger
2 to 3 tbs. olive oil	freshly ground pepper
4 cloves garlic, minced	2 green onions, thinly sliced
1 cup pale dry sherry	4 whole cloves
1/3 cup soy sauce	

Rub roast with about 1 tablespoon oil and the minced garlic. Place meat in a glass or stainless bowl. Add sherry, soy, ginger, pepper, onions and cloves. Turn meat to coat. Cover and chill overnight. To cook, remove meat from marinade. Save marinade. Pat meat dry with paper towels. Brown well on both sides in 1 to 2 tablespoons olive oil. Transfer to crockery pot. Add 1/2 cup reserved marinade. Cover. Cook on low (200°) 7 to 8 hours or until fork tender. Transfer to platter and keep warm. Add 1/2 cup more marinade to pan juices. Cook down until reduced. Pour into sauce bowl. Makes 8 to 10 servings.

GINGERED ROUND STEAK

Fresh ginger root and soy sauce permeate round steak creating a mahogany glaze.

2 lbs. round steak	3 tbs. soy sauce
2 inner stalks celery	1/3 cup red wine
4 green onions, chopped	1 tsp. freshly grated ginger
3 tbs. butter	1/4 lb. fresh mushrooms

Cut steak into servings. Slice celery diagonally into 1 inch pieces. Sauté celery and onions in 1 tablespoon of butter just until glazed. Turn out of pan and set aside. Add 1 more tablespoon butter to pan. Brown meat on both sides. Transfer to crockery pot. Add soy sauce and wine to frying pan. Stir to loosen brown bits. Pour over meat. Sprinkle with ginger root. Arrange sautéed vegetables on top. Cover. Cook on low (200°) 6 to 8 hours. Wash and slice mushrooms. Sauté in remaining butter. Add to meat the last half hour of cooking time. Makes 6 servings.

SAVORY SWISS STEAK

Vegetables thicken the rich sauce which smothers fork-tender steak.

1-1/2 lbs. round steak	1 onion, finely chopped
1/4 cup flour	2 carrots, peeled and grated
2 tsp. dry mustard	2 stalks celery, finely chopped
1 tsp. salt	1 can (16 oz.) tomatoes
1/4 tsp. pepper	2 tbs. Worcestershire sauce
2 tbs. each butter and oil	1 tbs. brown sugar

Cut steak into 6 serving-size pieces. Coat with a mixture of flour, mustard, salt and pepper. Using a large frying pan, brown meat in half the butter and oil. Transfer to crockery pot. Heat remaining butter and oil in frying pan. Sauté onion, carrots and celery until glazed. Add tomatoes, Worcestershire and brown sugar. Heat, scraping up drippings. Pour over meat. Cover. Cook on low (200°) 6 to 8 hours, or until tender. Serve meat with sauce spooned over. Sprinkle with parsley. Serves 6.

BEEF IN WALNUT SAUCE (Lagoto)

This unusual recipe for spiced beef in a nut sauce comes from Greece.

4 lb. rump roast, cut in cubes
seasoned flour
olive oil
1/2 cup water
1 can (8 oz.) tomato sauce
4 to 6 cloves garlic, minced

1/3 cup cider vinegar
1 whole cinnamon stick
8 <u>each</u> whole cloves and allspice
1 cup ground walnuts
1 tbs. lemon juice
sliced sourdough French bread, toasted

Dredge meat in seasoned flour. Shake off excess. Heat oil in large frying pan. Brown meat well. Transfer to crockery pot. Pour water into frying pan to loosen drippings. Add to crockery pot with tomato sauce, garlic and vinegar. Place cinnamon stick, cloves and allspice in a tea ball or cheesecloth. Add to pot. Cover. Cook on low (200°) 8 to 10 hours, or until very tender. If necessary, cook down pan juices. Add walnuts and lemon juice. Heat to serving temperature. Serve over hot buttered toast. Makes 12 servings.

BEEF STIFADO

Pickling spices and red wine vinegar punctuate this Greek stew. Round out the Aegean menu with pilaff, sesame-coated bread and a green salad with feta cheese.

2-1/2 lbs. lean stewing beef
3 tbs. butter
1 can (1 lb.) small onions
1 tbs. brown sugar
1/2 cup dry red wine
1/2 cup water
3 tbs. tomato paste
1/4 cup red wine vinegar
1 tsp. mixed pickling spices
4 whole cloves
3 cloves garlic, minced
1 tsp. salt
1 pkg. (12 oz.) frozen tiny peas

Cut meat in 1 inch chunks. Melt butter in large frying pan. Brown meat. Transfer to crockery pot. Stir drained onions and brown sugar into frying pan. Cook over medium high heat, shaking pan, until glazed. Transfer to crockery pot. Add wine, water, tomato paste and vinegar to frying pan. Stir to loosen drippings. Pour over meat and onions. Place pickling spices and cloves in a tea ball or cheesecloth bag. Add to pot. Season with garlic and salt. Cover. Cook on low (200°) 8 hours. Thaw peas. Add the last half hour of cooking. Cook down juices until slightly reduced. Serve in ramekins. Makes 8 servings.

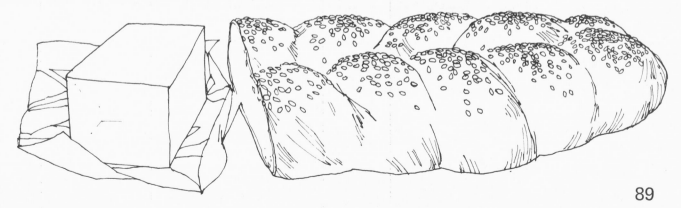

BEEF EN DAUBE

2 lbs. lean stewing beef
2 slices bacon, diced
2 doz. tiny boiling onions
1 tbs. each red wine vinegar and brown sugar
1-1/2 cups dry red wine
1-1/2 tsp. salt

1/2 tsp. each pepper and thyme
2 cloves garlic, minced
1 tsp. beef stock base
2 strips orange peel
2 tbs. cornstarch
2 tbs. chopped parsley

Cut meat in 1 inch cubes. Fry bacon until crisp. Remove from pan. Pour off all but 2 tablespoons drippings. Brown meat and onions in drippings. Transfer to crockery pot along with bacon. Add vinegar and brown sugar to pan drippings. Cook 1 minute, stirring. Pour in wine. Bring to a boil. Pour over meat. Season with salt, pepper, thyme, garlic, stock base and orange peel. Cover. Cook on low (200°) 8 hours. Turn to high (300°). Mix cornstarch with 1 tablespoon cold water. When pan juices are bubbling, stir in cornstarch paste. Cook, stirring until thickened. Garnish with parsley. Makes 6 servings.

SHORT RIBS PACIFIC STYLE

A soy sauce glaze penetrates the short ribs as they braise in the crockery pot.

3 to 4 lbs. beef short ribs, cut in 2 to 3 in. lengths
1 onion, chopped
1 tbs. butter
2/3 cup catsup
3 tbs. soy sauce
2 tbs. cider vinegar
2 tbs. brown sugar

Place short ribs on a broiler pan. Broil until well-browned to remove excess fat. Transfer to crockery pot. Sauté onion in butter until limp and golden. Pour in catsup, soy, vinegar and brown sugar. Heat until blended. Pour over ribs. Cover. Cook on low (200°) 8 hours. Makes 4 servings.

CORNED BEEF AND VEGETABLES

Here's another chance to cook for two meals at one time. Plan two appearances for corned beef. First, serve it hot with vegetables. For the second showing, make delicious Reuben-style sandwiches. Spread slices of rye bread with creamy Russian dressing, layer with corned beef, Swiss cheese and sauerkraut and grill in butter until cheese melts.

4 lb. corned beef brisket
3 carrots, cut in 3-in. pieces
2 stalks celery, cut in 2-in. pieces
2 medium onions, quartered

1 cup dry white wine
1 bay leaf
3 whole cloves

Wash brisket under cold running water to remove excess brine. Place in crockery pot. Add vegetables to crockery pot with wine, bay leaf and cloves. Cover. Cook on low (200°) 8 hours, or until tender. Transfer meat and vegetables to a heated platter. Pour juices into a sauce bowl. Makes 8 to 10 servings.

GLAZED SAUSAGE STRIPED MEAT LOAF

Potatoes cut "French fry" style bake around this juicy meat loaf.

3 (about 3/4 lb.) mild Italian sausages
2 eggs
1/2 cup milk
2 slices bread
1 tsp. <u>each</u> salt and Worcestershire
1 tsp. dry mustard
1 tsp. beef stock base
1 small onion
1-1/2 lbs. ground beef chuck
1/4 cup catsup
1 tsp. Dijon-style mustard
1-1/2 tbs. brown sugar
4 large boiling potatoes
2 tbs. soft butter

94

Simmer sausages in water to cover 10 minutes. Drain. Place eggs, milk, bread, salt, Worcestershire, dry mustard, stock base and onions in blender container. Cover. Blend until smooth. Place ground meat in mixing bowl. Pour in blender contents. Mix until smooth. Pat half of meat loaf mixture in the bottom of crockery pot. Cover with sausages. Top with remaining meat loaf. Pat to seal. Combine catsup, mustard, and brown sugar. Spread over meat. Peel potatoes. Cut in strips. Coat well with butter and place around meat. Cover. Cook on high (300°) 1 hour. Reduce to low (200°) 6 hours. Serves 8.

FLORENTINE MEAT BALLS

1 pkg. (10 oz.) frozen chopped spinach
3 eggs
2 slices fresh bread
2 tbs. minced parsley
1/4 cup grated Parmesan cheese
1-1/2 tsp. salt
1/4 tsp. pepper

1 clove garlic, minced
1-1/2 lbs. ground beef chuck
1/2 lb. bulk pork sausage
1 small onion, grated
flour
2 tbs. butter
Red Wine Sauce

Defrost spinach and squeeze dry. Beat eggs. Mix in bread, parsley, cheese, salt, pepper and garlic. Add meats, spinach and onion. Mix thoroughly to blend. Shape into 1 inch balls. Roll in flour. Brown in butter in large frying pan. Transfer to crockery pot. Pour in Red Wine Sauce. Cook on low (200°) 1 to 2 hours. Makes 6 to 8 servings.

Red Wine Sauce—Stir 1/2 cup each consommé and dry red wine into pan drippings after meat balls are browned. Boil until reduced to 1/3 cup. Add 1/2 teaspoon dried oregano. Use as directed.

96

SCANDINAVIAN MEAT BALLS

Delicious topped with sour cream or yogurt. Leftovers make fine sandwiches. Simply split and put between slices of buttered rye bread. Serve with dill pickles.

2 lbs. ground beef chuck
1/4 cup instant onion
2 eggs
1/2 cup quick-cooking oatmeal
2/3 cup milk
2 tbs. chopped parsley

2 tsp. beef stock base
1/2 tsp. salt
1/4 tsp. pepper
1/4 tsp. <u>each</u> nutmeg and allspice
1/2 cup beef broth <u>or</u> consommé
sour cream <u>or</u> yogurt

Place ground meat, onion, eggs, oatmeal, milk, parsley, stock base, salt, pepper, nutmeg and allspice in a mixing bowl. Mix until blended. Shape into 1-1/4 inch balls. Place 1 inch apart in a shallow baking pan. Bake in a 425°F oven 15 minutes, or until browned. Transfer to crockery pot. Pour in broth. Cover. Cook on low (200°) 1 to 2 hours. Serve with sour cream or yogurt. Makes 6 to 8 servings.

MEAT BALLS STROGANOFF

Toasted French bread slices make a great base for this creamy meat ball dish.

3 tbs. butter
1 medium onion, finely chopped
2 lbs. ground beef chuck
1 tsp. salt
1/4 tsp. pepper
1/4 each tarragon and basil
2 tbs. flour
1/3 cup tomato paste
3/4 cup canned consommé
2 tsp. Worcestershire
2 tsp. cider vinegar
1/2 lb. mushrooms, sliced
1 cup (1/2 pt.) sour cream
sliced French bread

Melt half the butter in large frying pan. Sauté onion until golden. Transfer to crockery pot. Quickly shape meat into bite-sized balls. Drop into frying pan. Sauté, shaking to turn, until browned. Sprinkle with salt, pepper, tarragon, basil and flour. Cook a few minutes. Transfer to crockery pot. Add tomato paste, consommé, Worcestershire and vinegar to frying pan. Stir to loosen drippings. Pour into crockery pot. Cover. Cook on high (300°) 1-1/2 to 2 hours. Sauté mushrooms in remaining butter. Add to meat balls along with sour cream. Heat thoroughly. Serve over toasted, buttered French bread. Makes 6 to 8 servings.

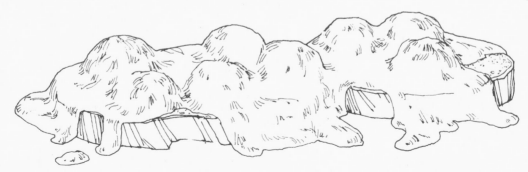

ITALIAN MEAT SAUCE

Spoon this sauce over tagliarini or spaghetti or use it in pasta dishes such as lasagne. Blended with ricotta cheese, it makes a choice filling for canneloni.

2 each onions and carrots
2 celery stalks
1/3 cup olive oil
2 lbs. ground beef chuck
1 lb. mild Italian sausage
3 cloves garlic, minced

4 tomatoes, peeled and chopped
1 cup dry red wine
2 tsp. dried basil
2 beef bouillon cubes
salt and pepper to taste
1/4 cup heavy cream

Grate onions and carrots. Finely chop celery. Sauté in oil in large frying pan until glazed. Transfer to crockery pot. Remove casings from sausage. Brown meats in frying pan. Crumble with a fork. Transfer to crockery pot. Add garlic, tomatoes, wine, basil and bouillon. Cover. Cook on low (200°) 8 hours. Skim fat. Season with salt and pepper. Stir in cream. Cook on high (300°) until reduced to desired consistency. Makes 8 to 10 servings.

GREEK-STYLE MEAT SAUCE

This meat sauce is great for various dishes: spaghetti, moussaka, and the Greek macaroni dish, Pastitsio. It is also good spooned over tacos or ladled inside avocado half shells. This recipe makes a quantity and freezes well.

4 lbs. ground beef chuck
2 tbs. butter
4 medium onions, finely chopped
4 cans (6 oz. each) tomato paste
4 cloves garlic, minced

1 tsp. mixed pickling spice
1 cup dry red wine
1 tbs. salt
freshly ground pepper

Using a large frying pan, brown meat in 1 tablespoon butter until it loses its pink color. Transfer to crockery pot. Add remaining butter to pan. Sauté onions until glazed. Transfer to crockery pot. Add tomato paste, garlic, pickling spice, (put in tea ball or tie in cheesecloth bag), wine, salt and pepper. Cover. Cook on low (200°) 8 hours. Stir once or twice. Cool slightly. Ladle into freezer containers, or serve hot. Makes about 3 quarts.

CALIFORNIA TOSTADAS

Tortillas pyramided with meat sauce and condiments are especially fun for a teenage gathering. The meat sauce freezes well so it can be made ahead.

Meat Sauce, page 103
salad oil
12 tortillas
condiments: hot refried beans
                shredded lettuce
                shredded Cheddar cheese
                chopped tomatoes
                sliced avocado

Prepare Meat Sauce. Just before serving time, heat 1/4 inch oil in large frying pan. Fry tortillas, one at a time, about 30 seconds on each side, or until slightly browned and crisp. Use tongs for handling hot tortillas. Drain on paper towels. Wrap loosely in foil and keep warm in low oven. Arrange condiments in bowls, tortillas in a basket and Meat Sauce in crockery pot. Let guests assemble their own tostadas by spooning refried beans onto tortillas first, then Meat Sauce, lettuce and remaining condiments. Makes 8 servings.

Meat Sauce—In a large frying pan sauté 2 chopped onions in 1 tablespoon butter until golden. Transfer to crockery pot. Brown 2 pounds ground beef chuck in frying pan. Transfer to crockery pot. (Use a slotted spoon for transferring meat to crockery pot so excess fat will be left in frying pan.) Season meat with 1 teaspoon salt, 2 minced cloves garlic, 1/2 teaspoon each ground cumin, oregano, and seasoned pepper. Add 1 can (6 oz.) tomato paste, 1/2 cup canned consommé, 1 tablespoon red wine vinegar and 2 teaspoons brown sugar. Cover. Cook on low (200°) 4 to 6 hours.

TOSTADA PIE

Good companions for this entree are Mexican beer, avocado and tomato salad and fresh pineapple wedges.

Meat Sauce, page 105
4 to 6 corn tortillas
1-1/2 cups (6 oz.) shredded Monterey Jack cheese
1/2 cup sour cream
2 green onions, chopped
2 tbs. soft butter

Prepare Meat Sauce as directed. Place a square of foil in bottom of crockery pot. Lightly butter one side of tortillas. Lay one tortilla, buttered side up, on foil. Spread with a layer of Meat Sauce and a layer of cheese. Cover with another tortilla, more Meat Sauce and cheese. Repeat layers ending with cheese. Cover. Cook on high (300°) 1 hour. When ready to serve, lift from crockery pot by foil corners. If desired, slip under broiler to brown cheese. Cut in wedges. Combine

sour cream and onions. Serve with Tostada wedges. Makes 4 to 5 servings.

Meat Sauce—Melt 2 tablespoons butter in large frying pan. Sauté 1 chopped onion until golden. Add 1 pound ground beef chuck, 1 teaspoon Mexican seasoning, 1/2 teaspoon salt, 2 cloves minced garlic and 1 can (8 oz.) tomato sauce. Cover. Simmer 30 minutes, or transfer to crockery pot and cook on low (200°) 8 hours. Mix in 1 cup sliced, pitted olives. Use as directed.

RAVIOLI CASSEROLE

1 pkg. (10 oz.) frozen chopped spinach
1 pkg. (8 oz.) twisty noodles
1 lb. ground beef chuck
1/2 lb. mild Italian sausage
1 onion, finely chopped
2 tbs. oil
2 cans (8 oz. each) tomato sauce

1 tsp. <u>each</u> salt and oregano
1/2 cup shredded Parmesan <u>or</u>
   Romano cheese
1 cup (1/2 pt.) sour cream
1 cup (4 oz.) shredded Monterey
   Jack cheese
3 green onions, chopped

Defrost spinach. Squeeze dry. Cook noodles in boiling salted water until tender. Drain. Brown meats and onion in oil until crumbly. Add tomato sauce, salt and oregano. Cover. Simmer 30 minutes. Mix in spinach. Spoon half the noodles into a buttered crockery pot. Top with half of meat mixture and Parmesan cheese. Cover with layers of remaining noodles, meat and Parmesan cheese. Spread with sour cream. Sprinkle with Jack cheese and onions. Cook on high (300°) 1 hour. Makes 8 servings.

Made and Boil
especially
For Lou S
Pappoo

VEAL AND APRICOTS TAJINE

The exotic influence of Morocco is evident in this spicy stew.

2 lbs. veal stewing meat
2 tbs. butter
1 tbs. olive oil
1 medium onion, finely chopped
2 tsp. freshly shaved ginger
1-1/2 tsp. salt
1 tsp. cumin

1/4 tsp. pepper
1 cinnamon stick
2 cloves garlic, minced
3/4 cup moist dried apricots
1/4 cup golden raisins
1 tbs. each honey and lemon juice
1/4 cup pine nuts (optional)

Cut veal into 1-1/4 inch cubes. Heat butter and oil in large frying pan. Sauté onion with ginger, salt, cumin, pepper and cinnamon until glazed and golden brown. Add garlic and meat. Brown well. Transfer to crockery pot. Add apricots and raisins. Cover. Cook on low (200°) 7 to 8 hours or until meat is tender. Add honey and lemon juice. Turn to high, (300°). Cook a few minutes longer. Garnish with pine nuts. Makes 6 servings.

VEAL STEW WITH ONIONS

Mixed pickling spice lends a novel fillip to this Greek veal stew.

2 lbs. veal stewing meat
seasoned flour
1 tbs. butter
1 tbs. olive oil
1/4 cup water
3 cloves garlic, minced

1/2 cup tomato sauce
2 tbs. red wine vinegar
1/2 tsp. whole mixed pickling spice
1 can (15 oz.) small whole onions
3 tbs. chopped parsley

Cut meat in 1-1/4 inch cubes. Roll in flour. Heat butter and oil in large frying pan. Brown meat. Transfer to crockery pot. Add water to pan drippings. Stir to loosen brown bits. Pour into crockery pot. Add garlic, tomato sauce, vinegar and mixed pickling spice, tied in a cheesecloth bag or tea ball. Cover. Cook on low (200°) 6 to 8 hours. Add drained onions. Heat to serving temperature. Sprinkle with parsley. Makes 6 servings.

TARRAGON VEAL STEW

Serve this wine-laced stew on a bed of pilaff. Garnish with toasted almonds.

2 lbs. veal stew
seasoned flour
3 tbs. butter
1 cup dry white wine
1 cup beef broth <u>or</u> stock
2 shallots, chopped

2 cloves garlic, minced
1 tsp. dried tarragon
1/2 tsp. grated lemon peel
2 tbs. heavy cream
1 tsp. lemon juice

Dust veal with seasoned flour. Melt 2 tablespoons butter in large frying pan. Brown meat well. Transfer to crockery pot. Pour wine and broth into frying pan. Stir to loosen pan drippings. Pour over veal. Add shallots, garlic, tarragon and lemon peel. Cover. Cook on low (200°) 8 hours. Ladle pan juices into saucepan. Boil down until reduced and slightly thickened. Stir in cream and lemon juice. Add remaining butter. Heat until blended. Return to crockery pot. Heat thoroughly. Makes 6 servings.

MOROCCAN LAMB CHOPS AND PRUNES

Fresh cilantro and ginger root are essential to the authenticity of this aromatic North African entree.

1 medium onion, finely chopped
2 tbs. butter
4 shoulder lamb chops
salt and pepper to taste
1-1/2 tsp. freshly shaved ginger

1/2 tsp. ground cumin
2 cloves garlic, minced
1 cinnamon stick
1 tbs. chopped cilantro
1 cup pitted prunes

2 tbs. honey
1-1/2 tbs. lime juice
2 tbs. toasted
    sesame seed

Using a large frying pan, sauté onion in butter until limp. Push to sides of pan. Brown chops well on both sides. Season with salt and pepper. Add ginger, cumin, garlic and cinnamon. Sauté 1 minute. Transfer to crockery pot. Rinse pan with 2 tablespoons water to loosen drippings. Add to pot. Scatter cilantro and prunes over lamb chops. Cover. Cook on low (200°) 6 hours. Stir in honey and lime juice. Heat to serving temperature. Sprinkle with sesame seeds. Makes 4 servings.

BURGUNDY LAMB SHANKS

Wine and vegetables produce a robust sauce for slow-cooked shanks.

4 (about 3-1/2 lbs.) lamb shanks
salt and pepper to taste
1/2 tsp. <u>each</u> grated lemon peel
   and oregano
2 cloves garlic, minced

2 tbs. chopped parsley
1 carrot and onion, peeled and chopped
1 tbs. butter <u>or</u> olive oil
1 cup dry red wine
1 bouillon cube <u>or</u> 1 tsp. beef stock base

Season shanks with salt, pepper, lemon peel and oregano. Place in crockery pot. Sprinkle with garlic and parsley. Sauté carrot and onion in butter in large frying pan. Transfer to crockery pot. Pour wine into frying pan. Add bouillon cube. Stir to loosen drippings. Pour over shanks. Cover. Cook on low (200°) 8 hours. If desired, drain juice into saucepan. Boil to reduce and thicken slightly. Makes 4 servings.

TURKISH LAMB AND PINE NUT BALLS

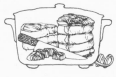

For a Middle Eastern dinner serve these nut-studded meat balls with hot Arabic bread, cucumber and yogurt salad, pilaff and steamed zucchini.

1-1/2 lbs. ground lean lamb
1/2 cup hot or cold mashed potatoes
1 egg
1/3 cup pine nuts
3 tbs. currants
2 tbs. minced parsley
1/4 tsp. allspice

2 cloves garlic, minced
1 tsp. salt
freshly ground pepper
1 tbs. oil or butter
1 medium onion, chopped
1 can (8 oz.) tomato sauce
1/4 cup dry red wine

Mix lamb, potatoes, egg, nuts, currants, parsley, allspice, garlic, salt and pepper together well. Shape into 1-1/4 inch balls. Heat oil in large frying pan. Brown meat balls on all sides. Transfer to crockery pot. Add onion to frying pan. Sauté until limp and glazed. Add tomato sauce and wine. Bring to boil. Pour over meat balls. Cover. Cook on low (200°) 1-1/2 to 2 hours. Makes 4 servings.

LAMB CURRY

2 lbs. boneless lamb
1 to 2 tbs. curry powder
2 tbs. bacon drippings
2 tart apples, peeled and diced
2 onions, chopped
1-1/2 tsp. freshly shaved ginger
2 tbs. flour
2 cloves garlic, minced
1 cup consommé

1 cup dry red wine
1 tsp. lemon juice
1 tsp. salt
hot steamed rice
condiments: toasted almonds
                  crisp bacon
                  chutney
                  chopped apple
                  chopped green onion

Brown meat and curry powder in bacon drippings in large frying pan. Transfer to crockery pot. Add apples, onions, ginger root and flour to frying pan. Cook until glazed. Transfer to crockery pot. Add garlic, consommé, wine, lemon juice and salt. Cover. Cook on low (200°) 8 to 10 hours. Serve over rice. Pass condiments. Makes 6 servings.

CHOUCROUTE GARNI

This Alsation sausage and sauerkraut dish makes a splendid one-dish meal. Dijon-style mustard is a "must" for a condiment.

1-1/2 qts. (about 3 lbs.) sauerkraut
2 slices bacon, diced
2 onions, finely chopped
4 to 6 regular or smoked pork chops
2 tart apples, peeled and diced
2 cloves garlic, minced

8 whole peppercorns
1 cup dry white wine
2 lbs. assorted sausages: mild Italian
   sausages, bratwurst, kielbasa, or a
   string of cocktail frankfurters

Place sauerkraut in strainer. Rinse under cold water. Drain well. Using a large frying pan, sauté bacon with onions and chops until meat is browned. Place sauerkraut and apples in crockery pot. Arrange chops and onions on top. Add garlic, peppercorns and wine. Cover. Cook on low (200°) 4 to 6 hours. Add sausages. Cook 1 hour longer. Makes 8 to 10 servings.

CASSOULET

This French country bean stew is a natural for a crockery pot as long slow cooking enhances the flavor.

1-1/2 cups small white or Great Northern beans
4-1/2 cups water
3 slices bacon, diced
2 medium onions, chopped
1 lb. each boneless lamb and pork shoulder, cut in 1-inch pieces
1 cup dry red wine
2 tbs. tomato paste
1/2 cup beef stock
1 carrot, peeled and grated
2 cloves garlic, minced
1 tsp. thyme
1 lb. mild Italian sausages

Soak beans overnight in water to cover. Drain. Simmer beans in 4-1/2 cups water 1 hour. Drain. Place in crockery pot. Sauté bacon and onions in large frying pan until golden. Transfer to crockery pot. Brown lamb and pork in remaining drippings. Transfer to crockery pot. Pour wine, tomato paste and stock into pan. Stir to loosen drippings. Add to crockery pot along with carrot, garlic, salt and thyme. Cover. Cook on low (200°) 6 to 8 hours. Add sausages. Cook 1 hour longer. Slice sausage on the diagonal. Arrange on top of casserole. Serve. Makes 8 to 10 servings.

PORK CHOPS IN ORANGE SAUCE

Pork chops gain a shiny rich glaze and tartness with this sauce.

4 thick center-cut pork chops
salt and pepper to taste
1 tbs. butter
1/3 cup <u>each</u> orange juice and catsup

1 tbs. orange marmalade
1/2 tsp. grated orange peel
1 orange, sliced
watercress for garnish (optional)

Season chops with salt and pepper. Brown well in butter in a large frying pan. Transfer to crockery pot. Pour orange juice and catsup into pan drippings. Stir in marmalade and orange peel. Boil 1 minute. Pour over chops. Cover. Cook on low (200°) 6 to 8 hours. Remove chops to warm platter. Slash orange slices to center. Twist and arrange one slice on each chop. Tuck a bouquet of watercress alongside. Pass sauce. Makes 4 servings.

119

SPINACH AND PORK TERRINE

Here is a brightly ribboned paté, stunning for a party appetizer or first course.

1 pkg. (10 oz.) frozen chopped spinach
3/4 lb. boneless pork, coarsely ground
1 egg
2-1/2 tbs. Cognac or brandy
2 tbs. chopped parsley
1/4 cup finely minced onion

1/2 tsp. each salt, thyme, and basil
1/4 tsp. each nutmeg and pepper
1/4 cup Italian-style olives, chopped
4 strips bacon
1/8 lb. sliced boiled ham
1 bay leaf

Thaw spinach. Squeeze dry. Place pork, egg, brandy, parsley and onion in mixing bowl. Combine salt, thyme, basil, nutmeg and pepper. Add half of seasonings to meat. Mix well. Mix remaining seasonings with spinach and olives. Line bottom and side of 4 by 7 inch loaf pan with bacon. Spread with 1/3 of meat mixture. Cover with half of spinach, half of the ham slices, another 1/3 of the meat, remaining spinach, ham, and meat. Place bay on top. Cover with foil. Cook in crockery pot on high (300°) 2 hours. Chill. Slice to serve. Makes 1 loaf.

COUNTRY-STYLE PATÉ

A 1-pound coffee can is the perfect container for baking this sausage-striped paté. Slice it into rounds and serve with sour dough bread as a first course.

3 mild Italian garlic sausages	2 tbs. brandy
1 lb. lean pork, coarsely ground	1 tbs. flour
2 slices bacon, ground	2 cloves garlic, minced
1 egg	1/2 tsp. grated lemon peel
2 tbs. sour cream	1/2 tsp. each salt and pepper
2 tbs. minced onion	1/4 tsp. each allspice and thyme

Place sausages in simmering water for 10 minutes. Drain and cool slightly. Mix together pork, bacon, egg, sour cream, onion, brandy, flour, garlic, lemon peel, salt, pepper, allspice and thyme. Butter a 1-pound coffee can. Spoon half the meat mixture into buttered can. Poke sausages in vertically. Spoon in remaining meat. Pat down. Cover with foil. Place in crockery pot. Cover. Cook on high (300°) 2 hours or until firm. Cool and chill. Makes 1 paté.

GLAZED HAM IN A BAG

Specially designed plastic cooking bags make neat containers for encasing roasts for crockery pot cookery. They seal all the flavorful juices around the roast and eliminate the need for clean-up.

5 lb. canned ham
3 tbs. orange marmalade
1 tbs. Dijon-style mustard

Remove ham from its can. Rinse off extra gelatin that clings to the meat. Place ham inside plastic cooking bag. Spread top of ham with a mixture of marmalade and mustard. Seal bag with twist-tie. Poke 4 holes in the top of bag. Place in crockery pot. Cover. Cook on low (200°) 6 to 8 hours. Transfer ham to carving board. Pour meat juices into a sauce bowl or pitcher. Skim off fat. Serve with ham. Makes 12 servings.

HAM LOAF WITH SWEET-SOUR GLAZE

This meat loaf is excellent hot or sliced cold for sandwiches.

2 cups ground cooked ham
1 lb. ground beef chuck
3/4 cup quick cooking oats
1 cup milk
2 eggs
1 tsp. dry mustard

1/2 tsp. <u>each</u> ground ginger and salt
1/4 tsp. <u>each</u> ground cloves and allspice
1/4 cup cider vinegar
1/4 cup firmly packed brown sugar
Mustard Sauce

Mix ham, ground beef, oats, milk, eggs, mustard, ginger, salt, cloves and allspice together. Shape into a loaf. Place on a square of foil. Put into crockery pot. Cover. Cook on high (300°) 2 hours. Meanwhile, boil vinegar and brown sugar in small saucepan until reduced by half. Cool. Spoon over loaf. Continue cooking 1 hour longer, or until cooked through. Serve with Mustard Sauce. Makes 8 servings.

Mustard Sauce—Blend 2 tbs. Dijon-style mustard into 1/4 cup sour cream.

SPAGHETTI CARBONARA

A crockery pot provides an ideal warmer-server for finishing off this renowned Italian pasta entree at the table.

1/4 lb. bacon, diced
1 bunch green onions, chopped
2 tbs. butter
2 egg yolks
1/2 cup finely chopped cilantro or parsley
1 cup diced Fontina or Gruyère cheese
2/3 cup shredded ham or proscuitto
1 lb. spaghetti, vermicelli, home-made noodles or fettucine
boiling, salted water
seasoned pepper
1-1/2 cups grated Parmesan cheese

Sauté bacon until crisp. Drain on paper towels. Pour off fat. Sauté onions in

124

butter until limp. Beat egg yolks. Have ready bowls of cilantro, bacon, Fontina cheese, ham and egg yolks. Cook spaghetti in boiling, salted water until al dente. Drain. Pour drained cooked spaghetti into preheated crockery pot. Mix in onion, bacon, cilantro, cheese, ham and egg yolks. Serve on heated plates. Pass seasoned pepper and grated Parmesan cheese. Makes 6 servings.

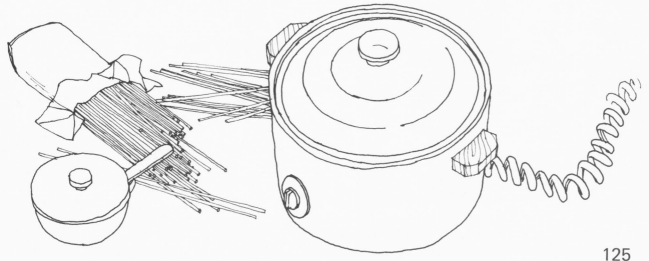

TONGUE IN PORT SAUCE

Cooked tongue is delicious glazed with a sprightly wine sauce. Cold, it is a pleasant change for the lunch box.

1 fresh _or_ smoked beef tongue
1 tbs. salt (omit for smoked tongue)
1-1/2 cups water
1 bay leaf

1 onion, quartered
6 whole peppercorns
Port Sauce

Place scrubbed tongue, salt, water, bay leaf, onion and peppercorns in crockery pot. Cover. Cook on low (200°) 7 to 9 hours. Remove from broth. Cool slightly. Skin using a sharp knife. Serve hot with sauce. Chill remainder for sandwiches. Makes about 12 servings.

Port Sauce—Combine in a saucepan 1/3 cup ruby port, 1 tablespoon currant jelly, 1 tablespoon lemon juice and 3/4 cup rich beef gravy (_or_ bouillon, plus 1 tablespoon cornstarch blended with 1 tablespoon cold water). Cook, stirring, until thickened. Makes 1 cup sauce.

126

SWEDISH LIVER LOAF

This Scandinavian paté makes a fine open-face sandwich on rye. Or pair it with other cold meats and a salad for luncheon.

1 lb. beef <u>or</u> calves liver, ground
1/4 lb. Italian garlic sausage
2 eggs
3/4 cup milk
1/2 cup crushed cracker crumbs

1-1/2 tsp. salt
1 tsp. <u>each</u> sugar, pepper and Worcestershire
1/2 tsp. allspice
1/4 tsp. <u>each</u> cinnamon, cloves,
   and <u>garlic</u> salt

Place ground liver, sausage, eggs, milk, cracker crumbs, salt, sugar, pepper, Worcestershire, allspice, cinnamon, cloves and garlic salt in a mixing bowl. Mix until blended. Pat into buttered 4 by 7 inch loaf pan. Cover with foil. Place in crockery pot. Cook on high, (300°) 2 to 2-1/2 hours or until firm. Let cool and chill. Slice to serve. Makes 1 loaf.

 ## ITALIAN SAUSAGES IN WINE

Sausages poached in red wine with a spoonful of currant jelly acquire a sensational flavor. Slice them thinly and pass as an appetizer, if you wish, or offer as a distinctive first course to prelude a quiche or cheese souffle supper.

6 to 8 mild Italian _or_ Polish sausages
1 cup dry red wine
2 tbs. currant jelly

Place wine and jelly in crockery pot. Heat until jelly is dissolved and sauce begins to simmer. Add sausages. Cover. Cook on high (300°) 45 minutes to 1 hour or until sausages are cooked through and lightly glazed. Transfer to a cutting board and slice thinly for a hot appetizer. Or serve individually in a ramekins with juices spooned over. Makes 6 first course servings or about 2 dozen appetizer servings.

GLAZED COCKTAIL FRANKS

A crockery pot makes a perfect warmer-server when entertaining. Try this easy appetizer for your next party.

1/4 cup Dijon-style mustard
1/2 cup dry red wine
3/4 cup currant jelly
1 lb. cocktail frankfurters

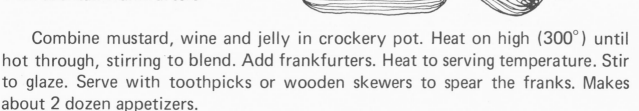

Combine mustard, wine and jelly in crockery pot. Heat on high (300°) until hot through, stirring to blend. Add frankfurters. Heat to serving temperature. Stir to glaze. Serve with toothpicks or wooden skewers to spear the franks. Makes about 2 dozen appetizers.

FRANKS IN SPICY TOMATO SAUCE

Here is a fast hot appetizer which is easy to assemble from ingredients generally on hand.

1 cup catsup
1/4 cup firmly packed brown sugar
1 tbs. red wine vinegar
2 tsp. soy sauce
1 tsp. Dijon-style mustard
1 clove garlic, minced
1 lb. frankfurters, cut in 1-inch pieces

Place catsup, brown sugar, vinegar, soy, mustard and garlic in crockery pot. Cover. Cook on high (300°) until blended. Stir occasionally. Add frankfurters. Cook until thoroughly heated. Makes about 4 dozen appetizers.

FETTUCINE ALFREDO

The Roman restaurant, Alfredo, makes a flourish of serving this pasta dish. Look for fresh egg noodles in the refrigerated section of your market.

1/3 cup butter
1 cup heavy cream
3/4 cup shredded Gruyère cheese
1 cup shredded Parmesan or Romano cheese
16 oz. fresh egg noodles
boiling salted water

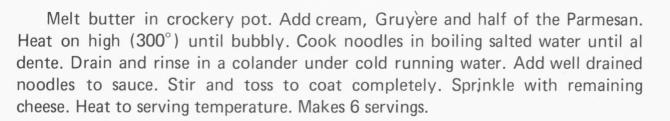

Melt butter in crockery pot. Add cream, Gruyère and half of the Parmesan. Heat on high (300°) until bubbly. Cook noodles in boiling salted water until al dente. Drain and rinse in a colander under cold running water. Add well drained noodles to sauce. Stir and toss to coat completely. Sprinkle with remaining cheese. Heat to serving temperature. Makes 6 servings.

BREADS AND CAKES

There are sometimes occasions when you may prefer not to heat the oven or perhaps you are at a location without an oven, when having a crockery pot makes baking possible.

Breads and cakes that steam or bake in a crockery pot have an excellent flavor, but a slightly coarser texture than if they had been oven-baked.

Before baking, select a mold or can that fits your crockery pot and is the correct size for the recipe you are using. A 1- or 2-pound coffee can fits any crockery-lined cooker. The larger models can also handle other container shapes such as a 2-1/2 quart pudding mold with a center tube, or 2 small loaf pans, about 4 by 7-1/2 inches, placed one on top of the other at right angles.

After you've enjoyed the following recipes, you may want to adapt some of your own favorites to the crockery pot method of cooking.

WHOLE GRAIN DATE BREAD

Slice this enriched date bread into rounds and spread with cream cheese.

1 cup boiling water
1 cup pitted dates, chopped
3 eggs
1 cup firmly packed brown sugar
1/2 cup all-purpose flour
1/2 cup whole wheat flour

1/4 cup wheat germ
1 tsp. baking powder
1/2 tsp. baking soda
1/2 tsp. salt
2 cups all-bran cereal
1 cup coarsely chopped pecans

Pour boiling water over dates. Cool. Beat eggs until light. Add sugar. Beat until thick. Stir in dates. Combine flours, wheat germ, baking powder, soda and salt. Add to egg mixture. Beat just until blended. Blend in cereal and nuts. Pour into well greased 1 pound coffee can. Place in crockery pot. Cover top of can with 4 layers of paper towels. Place crockery pot lid on loosely, allowing steam to escape. Cook on high (300°) 3 hours, or until a toothpick inserted comes out clean. Makes 1 large loaf.

ORANGE PECAN BREAD

Spread thin slices with sweet butter.

1/4 cup butter	1/2 tsp. salt
1 cup sugar	1 cup orange juice
1 egg	1 cup pitted dates, chopped
2 cups all-purpose flour	1/2 cup chopped pecans
1 tsp. <u>each</u> baking powder and soda	

Cream butter and sugar. Beat in egg. Combine flour, baking powder, soda and salt. Add dry ingredients to creamed mixture alternately with orange juice. Blend until smooth. Add dates and nuts. Turn into a greased and floured 2 pound coffee can. Place in crockery pot. Cover with 4 to 5 thicknesses of paper towels. Place crockery pot lid on loosely. Cook on high (300°) allowing 3-1/2 hours for 3-1/2 quart crockery pot and 4 hours for 4-1/2 quart size or until a toothpick inserted comes out clean. Cool on rack 10 minutes. Turn out of pan. Cool. Makes 1 loaf.

WHEAT GERM BROWN BREAD

Steam this moist brown bread in a 2 quart mold or a 3 pound coffee can.

1 cup whole wheat flour
1 cup all-purpose flour
1 cup yellow corn meal
1/2 cup wheat germ
1 tsp. each baking powder and soda
1 tsp. salt

1/2 cup firmly packed brown sugar
1/4 cup dark molasses
3 tbs. soft butter
2 cups buttermilk
1 cup golden raisins

Place flour, corn meal, wheat germ, baking powder, soda, salt and brown sugar in a mixing bowl. Stir until blended. Add molasses, butter and buttermilk. Beat until dry ingredients are moistened. Stir in raisins. Turn into a greased and floured 2 quart pudding mold or 3 pound coffee can. Pour 2 cups water into crockery pot. Place filled mold or can in pot. Cover top with foil, extending it to cover top of crockery pot. Cover. Cook on high (300°) 4 hours, or until a toothpick comes out clean. Makes 1 large loaf. This bread freezes well.

WHOLE WHEAT BANANA BREAD

Wheat germ and walnuts lend a nutty flavor to this moist fruit bread.

2/3 cup butter
1 cup sugar
2 eggs
1 cup pureed bananas
1 cup whole wheat flour

1 cup all-purpose flour
1/4 cup wheat germ
1/2 tsp. salt
1 tsp. baking soda
1/2 cup chopped walnuts or pecans

Cream butter with electric mixer. Add sugar. Beat until smooth. Add eggs and banana puree. Beat until smooth. Blend flour, wheat germ, salt and soda. Add to the creamed mixture. Beat just until smooth. Turn into a well-buttered 2 pound coffee can. Place in crockery pot. Cover coffee can with 4 paper towels. Place crockery pot lid on loosely to allow steam to escape. Cook on high (300°) 3-1/2 hours for small crockery pot models or 4 to 4-1/2 hours for large ones. Makes 1 loaf.

CHOCOLATE FILBERT CAKE

Mashed potatoes lend moistness to this old-fashioned chocolate nut cake.

2/3 cup butter
1-1/2 cups sugar
4 eggs
1 cup mashed potatoes
2 cups all-purpose flour

2/3 cup unsweetened cocoa
2 tsp. baking powder
1 tsp. each salt and cinnamon
1/2 cup milk
1/2 cup chopped filberts, pecans or walnuts

Cream butter. Beat in sugar and eggs until smooth. Mix in cooled potatoes. Combine flour, cocoa, baking powder, salt and cinnamon. Add dry ingredinets to creamed mixture alternately with milk. Add nuts. Turn into a greased and floured 3 pound coffee can or 3 quart pudding mold. Cover top of can with 4 layers of paper towels. Place crockery pot lid on loosely so steam can escape. Cook on high (300°) 3-1/2 to 4 hours or until a wooden skewer inserted in the cake comes out clean. Cool on cake rack 10 minutes. Remove cake from can. Makes 1 cake.

CHOCOLATE CHIP SOUR CREAM CAKE

A decorative mold works well for this delectably moist cake.

1/2 cup butter	2-1/2 cups all-purpose flour
1 cup sugar	1 tsp. baking powder
2 eggs	1 tsp. soda
1 cup (1/2 pt.) sour cream	1/2 tsp. salt
1 tsp. vanilla	1 pkg. (6 oz.) chocolate chips

Cream butter and sugar. Add eggs. Beat until smooth. Mix sour cream and vanilla. Stir flour, baking powder, soda and salt together. Add to creamed mixture. Stir in chocolate chips. Turn into well buttered and floured 2-1/2 to 3 quart mold or 3 pound coffee can. Place in crockery pot. Cover top of mold with 4 layers paper towels. Place crockery pot lid on loosely so steam can escape. Cook on high (300°) 4 to 5 hours or until a wooden skewer inserted in center comes out clean. Makes 1 large cake.

BEER SPICE CAKE

2/3 cup butter
1-1/2 cups firmly packed brown sugar
2 eggs
2-1/4 cups all-purpose flour
1-1/2 tsp. baking powder
1/2 tsp. soda

1/4 tsp. salt
1 tsp. <u>each</u> cinnamon and allspice
1 can (12 oz.) beer (1-1/2 cups)
1/2 cup <u>each</u> chopped walnuts and
    golden raisins

Cream butter and sugar until light. Beat in eggs. Combine flour, baking powder, soda, salt, cinnamon and allspice. Add dry ingredients to creamed mixture alternately with beer. Mix until blended. Stir in walnuts and raisins. Turn into well greased and floured 2 quart pudding mold or coffee can. Place in crockery pot. Cover top of can with 4 or 5 layers of paper towels. Place lid loosely on crockery pot. Cook on high (300°) allowing 3-1/2 hours for 3-quart pot and 4 hours for 4-1/2 quart size. Cool on rack 10 minutes, then turn out of pan. Serve warm with Hard Sauce, page 143, or ice cream. Makes 1 large cake.

MOROCCAN APPLESAUCE CAKE

Serve this unusual cake warm with scoops of coffee or chocolate ice cream.

1/2 cup butter	1-1/2 cups all-purpose flour
1 cup sugar	1 tsp. cinnamon
2 eggs	1/2 tsp. salt
1 tsp. vanilla	1 cup chocolate bits
1 cup applesauce	3/4 cup chopped dates or raisins
1-1/2 tsp. baking soda	3/4 cup chopped walnuts

Cream butter and sugar. Add eggs one at a time. Beat until smooth. Add vanilla. Combine applesauce and soda. Stir in. Mix flour, cinnamon and salt. Add to creamed mixture. Beat until smooth. Mix in chocolate bits, dates and walnuts. Turn into a greased and floured 2 quart pudding mold or 2 pound coffee can. Place in crockery pot. Cover with 4 layers of paper towels. Place crockery pot lid loosely on top so steam can escape. Cook on high (300°) 3 to 3-1/2 hours, or until a toothpick inserted in center comes out clean. Makes 1 large cake.

STEAMED CARROT PUDDING

This steamed pudding makes a gala finale to a holiday feast.

1 cup all purpose flour
1 cup firmly packed brown sugar
1 tsp. soda
1 tsp. <u>each</u> cinnamon and allspice
1/2 tsp. powdered cloves
1/3 cup soft butter
1 egg
1 cup grated carrots
1 cup grated apples <u>or</u> potatoes
1/2 cup golden raisins
Hard Sauce, page 143

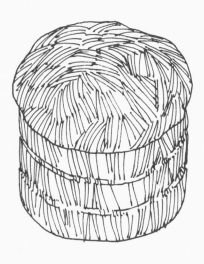

Place flour, sugar, soda, cinnamon, allspice and cloves in a mixing bowl. Stir to blend. Add butter and egg. Mix until smooth. Stir in carrots, apples and raisins.

142

Turn batter into well buttered and floured 2 quart coffee can. Pour 2 cups water into crockery pot. Set can of batter in water. Cover can with foil, and cover top of crockery pot with foil. Put lid on pot. Cook on high (300°) 4 to 5 hours, or until a tester inserted in center comes out clean. Serve warm with Hard Sauce. Makes 8 servings.

Hard Sauce—Beat 1/4 cup butter until creamy. Beat in 1-1/4 cups powdered sugar, 1 egg yolk and 1 tablespoon honey.

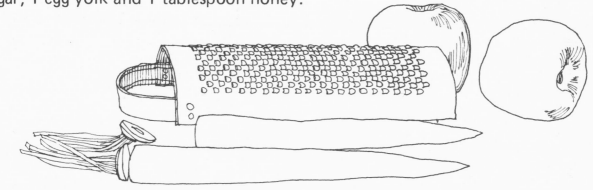

FRUITS

Fresh fruits poach or bake beautifully in a crockery pot and can be the basis for great desserts or everyday breakfast treats. The cooking time will vary with their ripeness and variety, so be sure to check the pot frequently (often by just peering through the see-through cover) to verify doneness.

Slowly cooked overnight, hot spicy fruit or freshly baked apples, served plain or with cream, are a big hit for breakfast. Even non-breakfast eaters will find this a combination hard to resist.

APPLES BAKED IN WINE

A rosy wine glaze makes a pretty sauce for plump baked apples.

4 Rome Beauty or Golden Delicious apples
1 orange
1/2 cup rosé wine
1/8 tsp. nutmeg
1/3 cup light brown sugar
whipped cream or ice cream for topping

Core apples. Peel off a ring around top. Arrange in crockery pot. Remove 2 strips orange peel with vegetable peeler. Cut orange in half. Squeeze out juice. Add peel, juice, wine, nutmeg and brown sugar to crockery pot. Cover. Cook on low (200°) 3 to 4 hours or until apples are fork tender. Cool. Serve with whipped cream or ice cream. Makes 4 servings.

CINNAMON SPICED APPLESAUCE

Tart, first of the season, Gravenstein or Pippin apples make superb applesauce.

8 to 10 large cooking apples
1/2 cup water
1/2 to 3/4 cup sugar
1 tsp. cinnamon
sweetened light cream

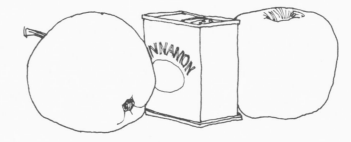

Peel, quarter and core apples. Place in a crockery pot. Add water and sugar. Sprinkle with cinnamon. Cover. Cook on low (200°) 8 hours (or on high (300°) 3 to 4 hours). Serve warm or cold with sweetened cream. Makes 8 servings.

APRICOTS AND CARAMEL CRUNCH SUNDAES

Caramelized almonds lend a crunchiness to this apricot dessert.

1 qt. fresh apricots, halved and pitted
1/4 to 1/2 cup firmly packed brown sugar
3 tbs. water
vanilla ice cream
Caramelized Almonds

Layer apricots in crockery pot. Sprinkle sugar between layers. Add water. Cover. Cook on low (200°) 1 to 2 hours or until apricots are just tender. Serve warm, spooned over scoops of vanilla ice cream. Top with Caramelized Almonds. Makes 6 to 8 servings.

Caramelized Almonds—Heat 2 teaspoons butter and 2 tablespoons sugar in frying pan until melted. Add 1/2 cup slivered _or_ sliced almonds, _or_ chopped filberts. Sauté, shaking pan until nuts are glazed with caramelized sugar. Turn out on foil to cool. Sprinkle over apricots and ice cream.

148

SHERRIED APRICOT COMPOTE

Apricots plumped in wine are refreshing over vanilla ice cream.

1 lb. dried apricots
2-1/2 cups water
1/4 cup brown sugar
1/2 cup pale dry sherry
1/2 cup golden raisins or currants
juice of 1 lemon
vanilla ice cream
1/4 cup slivered toasted almonds

Place apricots, water, sugar, sherry, raisins and lemon juice in crockery pot. Cover. Cook on low (200°) 3 to 4 hours or until fruit is plumped. Cool. Serve scoops of vanilla ice cream in dessert bowls. Spoon on sherried apricots. Sprinkle with almonds. Makes 6 servings.

POACHED BLUEBERRIES AND SOUR CREAM

If you are lucky enough to have freshly gathered huckleberries, this works beautifully for them as well.

1 cup sugar
1/2 cup water
3 slices lemon
1-1/2 pts. blueberries
1 tbs. Cointreau or undiluted orange juice concentrate
sour cream or whipped cream

Place sugar, water and lemon slices in crockery pot. Heat on high (300°) until sugar is dissolved and sauce comes to a boil. Add blueberries and simmer 15 to 20 minutes or until cooked through. Remove from crockery pot. Stir Cointreau into blueberries. Cool. Serve with sour cream or whipped cream. Makes 6 servings.

CHERRIES JUBILEE

If you like, flambé this gala cherry sauce at the table for a party dessert.

2/3 cup sugar
3/4 cup water
1-1/2 lbs. Bing cherries, pitted
2 tbs. currant jelly
2 tbs. kirsch or brandy
vanilla ice cream

Combine sugar and water in crockery pot. Heat on high (300°) until sugar is dissolved. Add cherries and jelly. Cover. Cook 15 to 20 minutes, or until fruit is tender. Baste occasionally. If you wish to flame the sauce, turn into heat-proof serving dish. Warm kirsch or brandy. Ignite and spoon flaming over cherry sauce. When flames go out, spoon sauce over vanilla ice cream which has been scooped into dessert bowls. Makes 6 servings.

 **GINGERED BAKED PAPAYA**

Hot spiced papaya makes an intriguing fruit accompaniment to roast chicken, duck or pork. It is a festive dessert as well, accompanied by pineapple or champagne sherbet.

1 large <u>or</u> 2 small papaya
3 tbs. butter
1-1/2 tbs. lime juice
2 tsp. freshly grated ginger root <u>or</u> 1/2 tsp. ground ginger

Cut small papaya in half. Quarter if large. Scoop out seeds. Combine butter, lime juice and grated ginger root in a saucepan. Heat until butter is melted. Arrange papaya in crockery pot. Spoon gingered butter in cavities of each. Cover. Cook on high (300°) 1-1/2 to 2 hours, or until tender. Baste once or twice with butter mixture. Serve hot. Makes 4 servings.

PEACHES ROMANOFF

1/2 cup sugar
3/4 cup water
2 whole cloves
6 peaches
1/4 cup brandy, Cognac, kirsch, Galliano, or orange-flavored liqueur

1/2 cup heavy cream
1-1/2 pts. rich vanilla ice cream
1/4 cup toasted slivered almonds or chopped filberts

Combine sugar, water and cloves in crockery pot. Heat on high (300°) until syrup is dissolved. Peel peaches. Add to syrup. Cover. Cook on high (300°) 15 to 20 minutes, or until tender. Baste occasionally. Turn out of crockery pot into a bowl. Stir in 2 tablespoons brandy or other liqueur. Cool and chill. Whip cream until stiff. Beat in remaining 2 tablespoons liqueur. Beat in slightly softened ice cream. Mix just until blended. Turn into freezer container. Cover. Freeze until firm. To serve, spoon 2 peach halves and syrup into each dessert dish. Top with a spoonful of ice cream sauce. Sprinkle with nuts. Makes 6 servings.

PEACHES MELBA STYLE

Poach fresh peaches and drench with raspberry sauce for a delectable dessert.

1 cup sugar
1-1/2 cups water
1 in. piece vanilla bean
6 large fresh peaches
1 pkg. (10 oz.) frozen raspberries, thawed
1 qt. vanilla ice cream

Place sugar, water and vanilla bean in a crockery pot. Heat on high (300°) until sugar is dissolved and syrup comes to a boil (allow about 45 minutes). Peel and halve peaches. Add to hot syrup. Simmer 15 to 20 minutes, or until fruit is tender. Remove from heat. Cool in syrup. Puree raspberries. Serve poached peaches in bowls with a scoop of ice cream on top of each. Pass raspberry sauce to pour over ice cream. Makes 6 servings.

RUBY PEARS

Baste pears occasionally so they absorb the wine juices and turn ruby red.

1 cup dry red wine
1/3 cup sugar
4 to 6 Bartlett or Bosc pears
4 to 6 cloves

Stir wine and sugar together in crockery pot. Heat on high (300°) until sugar dissolves. Remove cores from pears. Leave peel and stem intact. Stud each pear with a clove. Place in crockery pot. Cook on low (200°) 3 to 4 hours. (or high (300°) 1-1/2 to 2 hours). Baste. Serve warm or chilled. Makes 4 to 6 servings.

FRESH PLUMS IN PORT

Spicy wine flavors permeate poached plums thoroughly after chilling.

1 orange slice
4 whole cloves
1 qt. whole purple prune plums, slashed on 1 side to pit
1 cup ruby port
1/2 cup sugar
1 whole cinnamon stick

Quarter orange slice. Stud with cloves. Place in crockery pot with plums, port, sugar and cinnamon stick. Cook, uncovered, on high (300°) until sugar is dissolved. Turn temperature to low (200°). Cook 1 hour or until fruit just begins to soften. Transfer to a refrigerator container. Cover and chill. Makes 6 to 8 servings.

ORANGE-PLUMPED PRUNES

Cook prunes overnight, if you like, for a hot breakfast fruit.

1 lb. pitted large prunes
1 cup orange juice
1 cinnamon stick
1 lemon, thinly sliced

Place prunes, orange juice and cinnamon stick in crockery pot. Arrange lemon slices on top. If necessary add a little more juice or water to just cover prunes. Cover pot. Cook on low (200°) 8 hours or until plumped. Serves 6.

RHUBARB BERRY SAUCE

Accompany with light cream or ice cream for a refreshingly light fruit dessert.

2 cups fresh strawberries*
1 qt. thinly sliced rhubarb
3/4 cup sugar
3 tbs. minute tapioca

1 tsp. grated orange peel
1/4 cup water
light cream or ice cream

Wash and hull strawberries. Combine with rhubarb in lightly buttered crockery pot. Blend sugar, tapioca, orange peel and water together. Mix lightly with fruit. Let stand 15 minutes. Cover. Cook on low (200°) 3 to 4 hours or until just tender when pierced with a fork. Serve with light cream or ice cream. Makes 6 servings.

*or 1 pkg. (10 oz.) frozen whole strawberries, thawed

159

 **STRAWBERRY AND ORANGE SUNDAES**

Orange juice and ruby port are an old-time favorite with strawberries. For a shortcake-style dessert serve over slices of pound cake.

2 oranges, peeled
1 can (6 oz.) frozen orange juice concentrate
1-1/4 cups ruby port
2 cups hulled strawberries
1 qt. vanilla ice cream

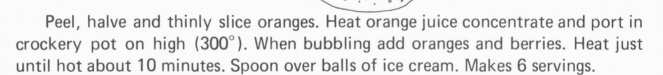

Peel, halve and thinly slice oranges. Heat orange juice concentrate and port in crockery pot on high (300°). When bubbling add oranges and berries. Heat just until hot about 10 minutes. Spoon over balls of ice cream. Makes 6 servings.

Note: When strawberries are out of season substitute 6 oranges instead.

SUMMER FRUIT COMPOTE

A medley of late summer fruits are poached in lemon-scented honey for this colorful dessert.

12 plums	1/2 cup each sugar and water
2 peaches	1 tbs. each honey and lemon juice
6 apricots	1 lemon, thinly sliced
1/4 lb. Thompson seedless grapes	yogurt, sour cream or light cream

Wash, halve and seed plums, peaches and apricots. Wash and stem grapes. Combine sugar and water in saucepan. Bring to a boil. Cook until sugar is dissolved. Stir in honey and lemon juice. Place prepared fruit in crockery pot. Add syrup. Arrange lemon slices on top of fruit. Cover. Cook on low (200°) for 6 hours (or 1-1/2 to 2 hours on high (300°). Let cool slightly before serving, or chill. Serve in bowls. Pass yogurt, sour cream or light cream. Makes 6 servings.

PRESERVES

Put nature's bounty from orchard and garden into your crockery pot. Cook long and slow for richly-flavored preserves. The real joy of making jams and butters the crockery pot way is that they simmer to the proper consistency without scorching and without the need for frequent stirring. There is no easier way to capture that wonderful old-fashioned flavor like Grandma's cooking used to have. Jams, conserves, marmalades, chutney and fruit butters are all rewarding treasures superbly made by gentle crockery pot cooking. Enjoy the recipes offered here and also adapt your own favorites to this method. Thicker preserves can be achieved by cooking several hours on low with the cover removed.

CIDER APPLE BUTTER

Brown sugar lends a caramelized richness to this smooth apple butter.

5 lbs. cooking apples
1-1/2 cups apple cider
brown sugar (about 3 cups)
juice and grated peel of 1 <u>each</u> lemon and orange

2 tsp. cinnamon
1 tsp. allspice
1/4 tsp. <u>each</u> cloves and nutmeg

Core and quarter apples, but do not peel. Place in crockery pot with apple cider. Cook on high (300°) until very soft, about 1-1/2 hours. Press cooked apples through a food mill or sieve. Measure. (There should be about 6 cups.) For every 1 cup fruit pulp, allow 1/2 cup brown sugar. Return to crockery pot. Stir in lemon and orange peel and juice, cinnamon, allspice, cloves and nutmeg. Cover. Cook on high (300°) until thick and dark, about 4 hours. Immediately pour into hot, sterilized glasses and seal. Makes about 8 cups.

ORANGE MARMALADE

When winter Navel oranges are at their prime, use them for this beautiful bright orange marmalade.

6 oranges	1/2 cup lemon juice
water	6 cups sugar

Remove peeling from 4 oranges. Place in a saucepan. Cover with water and simmer 30 minutes. Lift out cooked peel. Reserve water. Using a spoon scrape off the white tissue from cooked peel and discard. Slice and chop orange peel. Peel the remaining 2 oranges and thinly slice all 6 oranges. Place sliced oranges, peel and reserved water in crockery pot. Add lemon juice and enough additional water to cover just two-thirds of fruit. Cover. Cook on high (300°) 1 hour. Measure. Turn off heat. Stir in sugar (allow 2 cups sugar for each pint fruit). Let stand 2 hours. Stir occasionally. Without covering pot, bring mixture to a boil on high (300°). Boil until it reaches the jelly stage (it will sheet from a spoon), about 15 minutes. Ladle into hot sterilized glasses and seal. Makes about 5 pints.

PEACH AND PLUM CONSERVE

Blanched almonds lend a nutty crunch to this amber jam.

6 cups peach pulp
1-1/2 cups plum juice and pulp
1 cup crushed pineapple
6 cups sugar
1/2 cup slivered blanched almonds

Place peach pulp, plum pulp, pineapple and sugar in crockery pot. Cook on high (300°) uncovered, until thick and clear. Add nuts. Cook 5 minutes longer. Pour into hot sterilized jars and seal. Makes about 9 cups.

APRICOT PINEAPPLE JAM

Pineapple lends a delightful sweetness to contrast with the tang of apricots in this classic jam.

2-1/2 lbs. fresh apricots (about 7 cups sliced)
1 can (15 oz.) crushed pineapple
5 cups sugar

Wash and slice apricots. Place in crockery pot with pineapple and sugar. Cook on high (300°), uncovered, until thickened. Stir occasionally. Allow about 1 to 2 hours cooking time. Ladle into hot sterilized jars. Makes about 9 cups.

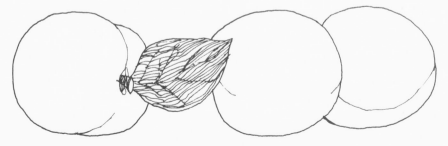

RHUBARB STRAWBERRY JAM

This jam is a beautiful color. Spoon it over toasted English muffins for breakfast.

2 lbs. rhubarb
6 cups sugar
2 lbs. strawberries (4 cups, mashed)

Wash rhubarb. Cut into 1/2 inch pieces. Place in crockery pot. Cover with sugar. Let stand 2 to 3 hours. Turn crockery pot to high (300°) and bring to boiling point. Add berries. Cook just until thickened, about 15 minutes. Ladle into hot sterilized jars. Makes about 4 pints.

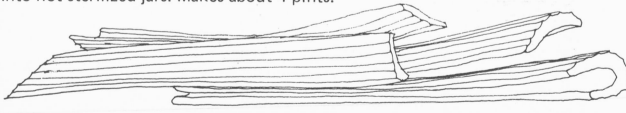

BRANDIED PEACHES

Peaches canned with a little brandy make a special meat accompaniment for a holiday dinner. Or flame them with additional brandy for a gala dessert.

5 lbs. peaches
3 cups sugar
2 cups water
3 tbs. lemon juice
1/2 cup brandy (approximately)

Peel, halve and pit peaches. Place sugar, water and lemon juice in crockery pot. Heat on high (300°). When simmering, add peaches. Simmer 15 minutes, or until peaches are tender. Pack into hot sterilized pint jars. Pour in syrup, allow ample head room. Spoon about 2 tablespoons brandy into each pint jar. Fill jar with syrup to within 1/2 inch of top. Seal. Makes about 5 pints.

APRICOT CHUTNEY

This colorful chutney is delicious with lamb curry, roast duck or turkey.

1 qt. ground ripe apricots
2 cups firm ripe apricots, chopped
1 large onion, grated
10 cloves garlic, minced
1 cup vinegar
1 can (8 oz.) crushed pineapple
2 tsp. salt
1-1/2 cups firmly packed brown sugar

2 tsp. dry mustard
1 tsp. cinnamon
1/2 tsp. each cloves and allspice
dash cayenne
1 tsp. grated lemon peel
1/3 cup sliced crystallized ginger
3/4 cup slivered blanched almonds

Place apricots, onion, garlic, vinegar, pineapple, salt, sugar, mustard, cinnamon, cloves, allspice, cayenne, lemon peel and ginger in crockery pot. Cover. Cook on low (200°), stirring occasionally, 4 to 6 hours. Remove cover. Add nuts. Cook on high (300°) until desired consistency. Ladle into hot sterilized jars. Seal. Makes 4 pints.

GINGERED PLUM CHUTNEY

Here is another sprightly fruit chutney, so good with game and broiled or curried meats.

1 qt. fresh Italian prunes
1 cup sugar
1 cup firmly packed light brown sugar
3/4 cup cider vinegar
1-1/2 tsp. crushed red peppers

2 tsp. <u>each</u> salt and mustard seed
3 cloves garlic, minced
1/4 cup grated onion
1/2 cup thinly sliced preserved ginger
1 cup golden raisins

Halve and pit prunes. Place sugars, vinegar, peppers, salt, mustard seed, garlic, onion, ginger and raisins in crockery pot on high (300°) until sugar is dissolved. Add prunes. Cook on low (200°) 4 to 6 hours. Stir occasionally. If desired, remove cover and cook down to desired consistency. Ladle into hot sterilized jars and seal. Makes about 3 pints.

BEVERAGES

A stoneware-lined, slow electric cooker works admirably as a beverage warmer-server for a crowd. A crockery pot filled with hot spiced cider, mulled wine, buttered sherry or Swedish Glugg is festive and practical for a wintertime party. Guests can serve themselves at will and the hot beverage stays at a perfect temperature without the hostess's attention. Conveniently prepared ahead of time, the flavor even improves as the ingredients slowly steep together.

DILLED TOMATO COCKTAIL

Dill pickle juice punctuates this quick tomato beverage.

3 cups tomato juice
2 tbs. sugar
1/2 tsp. celery salt
1 clove garlic, minced
1 tbs. Worcestershire sauce
dash liquid hot pepper seasoning
1/2 cup dill pickle juice
popcorn or croutons

Combine tomato juice, sugar, celery salt, garlic, Worcestershire sauce, hot pepper seasoning and pickle juice in crockery pot. Heat on low (200°) 1 to 2 hours. Ladle into mugs. Sprinkle a few kernels of popcorn on each. Makes about 6 to 8 servings.

CITRUS SPICED TEA

Hot citrus-scented tea is a welcome beverage for a winter afternoon party.

3 qts. water
1/3 cup tea leaves
1-1/2 cups sugar
1 tbs. whole cloves
1 tsp. whole allspice
2 sticks whole cinnamon
4 lemons
3 oranges

Heat 2 quarts water to boiling. Remove from heat. Add tea. Cover and steep 10 minutes. Strain into crockery pot. Add sugar, cloves, allspice and cinnamon. Heat on low (200°) until sugar is dissolved. Remove peel from 2 lemons and 2 oranges with a vegetable peeler. Add to pot. Squeeze juice from fruit. Strain and pour into pot. Add remaining water. Heat until steaming hot. Makes 24 servings.

HOT SPICED CIDER

Here is a spicy mulling of cider, wine and oranges.

1/2 gal. apple cider
2 cups sauterne or mellow white wine
4 oranges, sliced
2 sticks cinnamon
12 whole cloves

Place apple cider, wine, oranges, cinnamon and cloves in crockery pot. Cover. Heat on low (200°) until hot. To serve, remove cover and ladle into heat-proof punch cups. Makes about 24 servings.

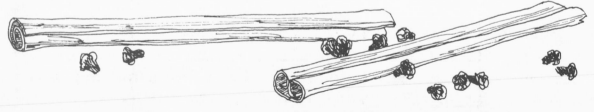

SWEDISH GLUGG

Typical of Scandinavian festivities is this richly spiced wine punch. In Sweden it is traditional to ignite a large lump of sugar and brandy and let it flame into the hot wine.

1 gal. port wine
1 to 2 cups brandy or bourbon
1 tbs. whole cloves

1 tbs. cardamom seeds, peeled
3 to 4 cinnamon sticks
1 cup dark raisins

Place port and brandy in crockery pot. Wrap cloves, cardamom seeds and cinnamon sticks in cheesecloth. Add to pot. Stir in raisins. Heat on low (200°) until steaming hot. Makes about 32 servings.

Note: Any remaining Glugg may be poured into jars or wine bottles and stored in the refrigerator for future use.

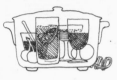 **HOT MULLED WINE**

Another Swedish variation of hot wine punch is based on dry red wine. You have the option of using either vodka or brandy for the spirits.

1-1/2 cups sugar
3 cups water
1 cinnamon stick
6 cardamom pods, peeled
12 whole cloves
1/2 cup golden raisins

1/4 cup blanched almonds
1/4 in. piece ginger root (optional)
1 lemon, thinly sliced
1/2 gal. dry red wine
1 to 2 cups vodka or brandy

Combine sugar and water in saucepan. Bring to a boil. Heat, stirring, just until sugar is dissolved. Pour into crockery pot. Add cinnamon stick, cardamom pods, cloves, raisins, almonds, ginger root, lemon, wine and vodka or brandy. Heat on low (200°) until steaming hot. Ladle into heat-proof punch cups or mugs. Be sure each cup gets an almond and a few raisins. Makes about 24 servings.

HOT BUTTERED SHERRY

Cinnamon sticks make natural stirrers in this hot wine drink.

1 can (6 oz.) frozen orange juice concentrate, undiluted
1 cup dry sherry
2 cups water
1 tbs. sugar
1 stick cinnamon
4 whole cloves
2 tbs. butter
cinnamon sticks for stirrers

Thaw orange juice concentrate. Combine concentrate, sherry, water, sugar, cinnamon stick and cloves in crockery pot. Cover. Heat on low (200°) 1 to 2 hours (or longer). Ladle into mugs. Top each with 1/2 teaspoon butter. Serve with a cinnamon stick in each mug. Makes 6 servings.

INDEX

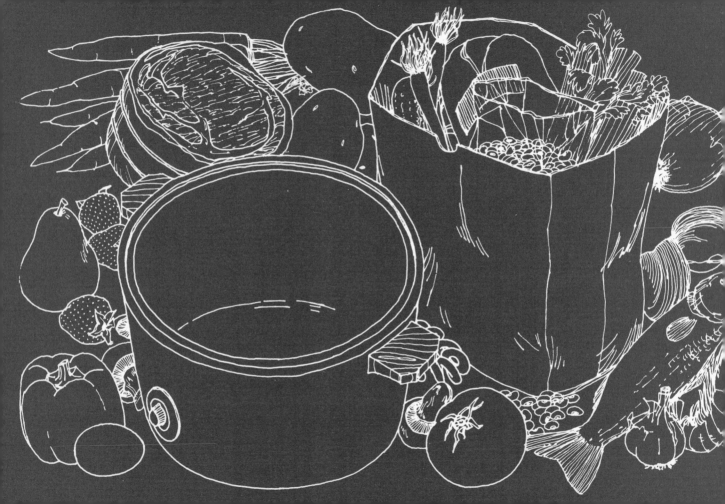